CW01647707

Lights, C

Merton!

The Films of Merton Park Studios

by

Clive Whichelow

To Kat

Thanks for all your help.

Published by

Enigma Publishing

4 Charnwood Avenue

London SW19 3EJ

Copyright © Clive Whichelow

All rights reserved. No part of this publication may be stored, reproduced or transmitted without the prior written permission of the author.

First edition September 2019

ISBN 978-0-9524297-4-6

Printed by Aquatint

Front cover: Merton Park film studios being visited by Konga, who was created here in 1961

CONTENTS

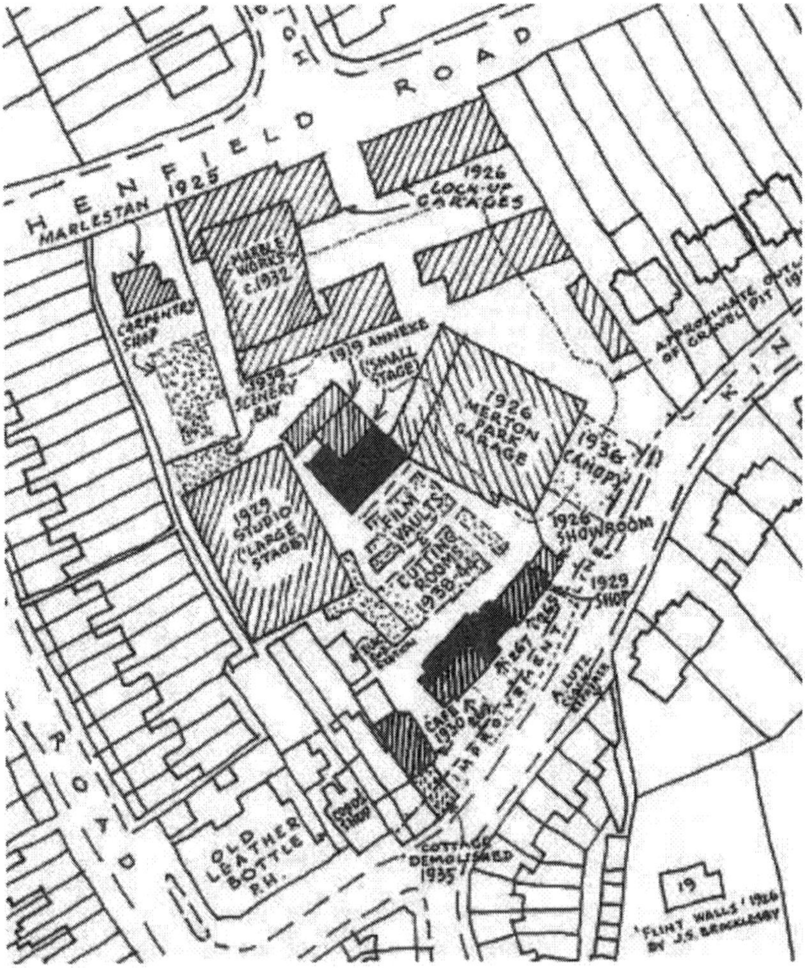

Merton Park studios layout by John Wallace – courtesy of the John Innes Society

INTRODUCTION

Over the years people have been rather disparaging about Merton Park film studios, associating them with low-budget B films and little-known actors. Of course, no Hollywood blockbusters were made there, but then that's what Hollywood is for. Small studios such as Merton Park were producing large numbers of the films that were necessary for cinemas to have a complete programme to show the viewing public. Yes, they were often B films, but some good feature-length films were made too, and many of those B films were better than they needed to be simply to fill the time before the main event. In January 1965 Daily Cinema magazine said of Merton Park's Act of Murder: 'Roll out the red carpet and hang out the flags for here is a second feature that puts much of the major stuff to shame.' In 1963 Kine Weekly's award for Best Second Feature Series went to Merton Park's Edgar Wallace series.

Perhaps one reason that people have been disparaging about Merton Park's output is that they simply do not know what was produced there, or by whom.

Some of the biggest names in cinema have worked at Merton Park film studios – Peter Sellers, Michael Caine, Richard Attenborough, Michael Winner, Diana Dors, Petula Clark, David Hemmings, Stanley Baker and also many others who, although not as well-known internationally, are household names in Britain. John Thaw, Joan Littlewood, Barbara Windsor, Spike Milligan, Rita Tushingham, Harry H Corbett, and many, many more. In addition to these perhaps the biggest name in British cinema history, J Arthur Rank, began his career here. Oh, and a Disney film was made here as well. Who knew?

Over the years there have been occasional articles about the studios in newspapers and magazines which, although welcome, have built up a few myths about the place. These are looked at in more detail in the 'Myths' section of this book.

It is perhaps for the Edgar Wallace, Scotland Yard, and Scales of Justice series that the studios are best remembered. These short, low-budget crime films were used as B pictures at the cinema in the 1950s and 60s and have often been shown on TV since, right up to the present day.

In addition to these, Merton Park also produced many full-length feature films including quite a number of horror films, one of them being Konga, the British answer to King Kong. Rather than terrorising the streets of Manhattan, Konga rampaged along Croydon High Street, though some of the scenes were shot in Kingston Road directly opposite where the studios stood.

The film studios opened at Long Lodge in Kingston Road in 1929, but they were the successors to studios that had been in nearby Quintin Avenue since 1913 when set up by James Howard Martin who had worked with British cinema pioneer Robert William Paul. Publicity Films had used the Quintin Avenue studios but had moved to Long Lodge by 1931.

In that same year Sound Services Ltd took over Publicity Films. The company had been set up by US company Western Electric in 1928 with the advent of 'talkies' and a view to making documentaries.

The studios were actually behind Long Lodge, where Clara and Rose, the sisters of Arts and Crafts architect John Sydney Brocklesby had run a school. Brocklesby left Long Lodge in 1937. The stage had originally been put up with a view to commercial and industrial usage but was turned into film and sound recording studios by Sound Services in 1931. A small stage had previously been the studio of pre-Raphaelite artist Frederic Shields who had lived and worked at Long Lodge from 1896 until his death in 1911.

In the early 1930s producer Julius Hagen of Twickenham studios used Merton Park studios for some overflow production work. For example, a comedy entitled The Admiral's Secret (1934), directed by Guy Newall and starring Edmund Gwenn and James Raglan, used both studios.

Early films made at Merton Park were mainly documentaries, advertising films or public information shorts.

In 1937 a new company called Merton Park Studios Ltd was formed with a capital of £100 in one pound shares. Also in that year Marlestan Cottage in Henfield Road was bought and used as part of the business. It was a flint cottage built by Brocklesby.

Film production continued through the war years; indeed, some of the films made here were for government information or propaganda purposes and occasionally stars of the day such as Stanley Holloway would turn up in them. Promotional films were made here for Ford Motors, Spillers pet foods, Dunlop, Persil and other well-known brands.

In the 1943 war comedy Schweik's New Adventures, directed by Karel Lamac, the part of a railway worker is played by a young Richard Attenborough. Also in that year the cutting rooms were expanded to help meet the increased workload.

In 1945 an English language dubbed version of the Russian comedy Volga Volga was made here and featured the voice of Trevor Howard.

After the war, entertainment films were made at Merton Park, such as the children's stories Jean's Plan (1946), Circus Boy (1947) and The Secret Tunnel (1947). A short educational film for children, Trouble At Townsend (1946) starred a very young Petula Clark.

By 1949 they were making feature films aimed at adults such as The Fool and the Princess, directed by William C Hammond and based on the story by Stephen Spender. The cast included Irene Handl. Also in 1949 the Case of Charles Peace was filmed here starring Michael Martin-Harvey and directed by Norman Lee.

Over the 1940s the studios had moved on apace, and in August 1944 the Film Producers Guild was formed. This was an amalgamation of seven separate documentary-making companies, Merton Park Studios Ltd, Sound Services Ltd, Publicity Films Ltd, Verity Films Ltd, Greenpark Productions Ltd, Gryphon Films and Technical Film Productions. Important documentary makers such as Paul Rotha, Peter Morley, John Grierson and Humphrey Jennings worked at the Guild early in their careers.

In 1948/49 the studios had expanded and added 'star' dressing rooms, 'crowd artiste' rooms and make-up rooms as well as a canteen and a film library. Apart from the work done in the studios, Merton Park also had twenty mobile units which were sent out to schools, offices and factories to show films they had made.

So, by the end of the 1940s the studios were very busy and still expanding, but the films they were to become best known for, The Edgar Wallace, Scales of Justice and Scotland Yard series – as well as many other full-length feature films, were still to come.

Surprisingly, J Arthur Rank, the biggest name in British cinema history, began his involvement in films at Merton Park Studios, starting with Mastership (1934).

In the 1950s the studios produced many films, often with a crime theme, for example, The Dark Man (1951) starring Maxwell Reed and William Hartnell, Mystery Junction (1951) with Sydney Tafler, and Counterspy starring Dermot Walsh and Hazel Court. There were also romantic films such as Hindle Wakes (1952) starring Leslie Dwyer, comedies such as The Great Game with Diana Dors and Thora Hird, and the Goons' Case of the Mukkinese Battlehorn, as well as horror films such as The Headless Ghost and Horrors of the Black Museum (both 1959).

The 50s also saw the start of one of Merton Park's well-known crime series: Scotland Yard which ran from 1953–1961. This was followed by the Scales of Justice series (1962–67), and the Edgar Wallace mysteries (1960–65).

The production of feature films continued apace during the 60s with a range of genres being represented. The Criminal (1960) starred Stanley Baker, Joan Littlewood's rambunctious comedy Sparrows Can't Sing (1962) starred James Booth and Barbara Windsor, and there were further films in the horror/sinister genre such as Devil Doll (1963) and the Frozen Dead (1966). There was also an early gay film, The Leather Boys (1964) starring Rita Tushingham and the sci-fi film Invasion (1966) starring Yoko Tani.

Despite stories of the studio's 1967 demise there were a couple of interesting films made here in the early 1970s: Crucible of Horror (1971) and Horror Hospital (1973), both starring Michael Gough.

The children's films also continued through the 1950s and 60s and finished in the early 70s with Egghead's Robot (1970) and The Troublesome Double (1971) both starring Keith Chegwin and Richard Wattis.

For further information regarding films made here after 1967 see the separate chapter towards the end of this book.

ACTION

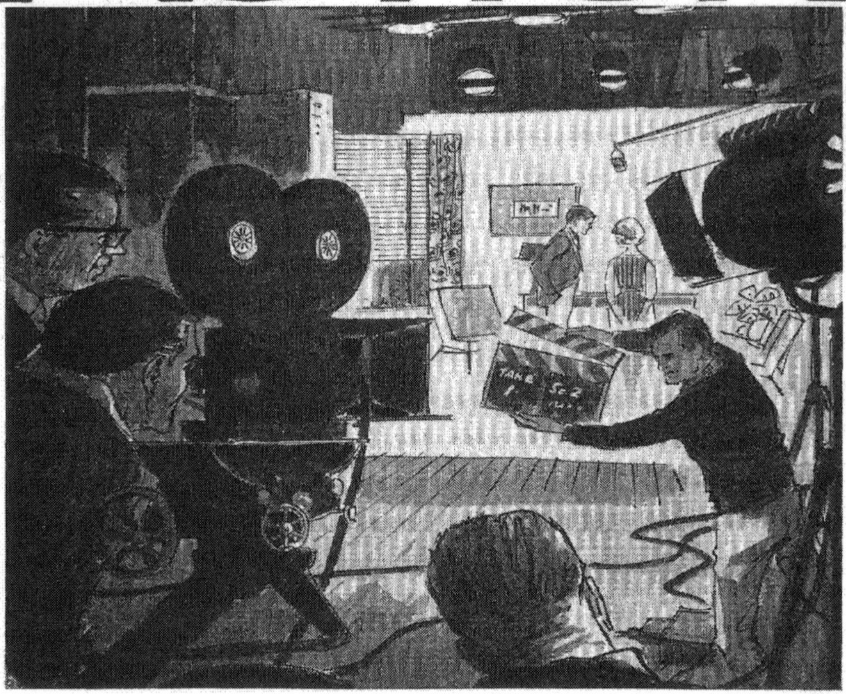

...IS THE KEY TO

MERTON PARK STUDIOS

For economy and every facility
for the complete production
of films from TV Commercials
to full length features

MERTON PARK STUDIOS LTD *(An Associate of The Film Producers Guild Ltd)*
269 KINGSTON ROAD SW19 TELEPHONE: LIBERTY 4291

M25

MASTERSHIP (aka the Mastership of Christ – 1934)

Directed by Aveling Ginever

Screenplay by Aveling Ginever

Starring: Gordon Bailey, Vi Caley, Henry Hepworth, Kathleen Joyce

This was the film that effectively started J Arthur Rank's illustrious film career. Although only twenty minutes long it included over a hundred actors and actresses in the crowd scenes and also the Poplar Methodist clergyman and politician William Henry Lax.

Rank was a Methodist and had taken over his father's flour business (later Rank Hovis McDougall). Since sound films – 'talkies' – had started (The Jazz Singer was 1927) he wanted to make religious films and so started the Religious Film Society.

He was a Sunday school teacher and thought there should be religious films of as good quality as those for cinema but when he couldn't find any decided to make his own.

Mastership (April 1934) was the first and had the alternative title The Mastership of Christ.

By July 1934 Rank had formed a company called British National Films.

In 1935 BNF became a commercial film company and in the same year Rank opened Pinewood studios with Lady Yule of Bricket Wood and film producer John Corfield.

By the following year he had become involved in film distribution due to the stranglehold the Americans had on the market.

In 1938 he bought the Odeon cinema chain and Elstree studios.

By 1942 Rank owned 619 cinemas.

Pinewood was where the Carry On, Superman and James Bond series were all later made.

In 1968 Rank refused to distribute Ken Russell's Women In Love due to some controversial scenes such as the nude wrestling. Ironically, this was partly filmed at Merton Park studios where Rank first became involved in the film industry (see section on films made after 1967).

THE ADMIRAL'S SECRET (1934)

Directed by Guy Newall (The Boat From Shanghai, The Chinese Puzzle)

Screenplay by Terence Egan (from the play by Cyril Campion and Eric Dignon)

Produced by Julius Hagen

Starring: Edmund Gwenn, Aubrey Mather, James Raglan, Edgar Driver

A farce involving retired admiral FitzPorter (Gwenn) who has stolen a rare diamond and is being pursued for it by a gang of Spanish criminals. There is also a death curse on the gem.

Notes: this was partly filmed at Twickenham studios which also used Merton Park for some overflow work.

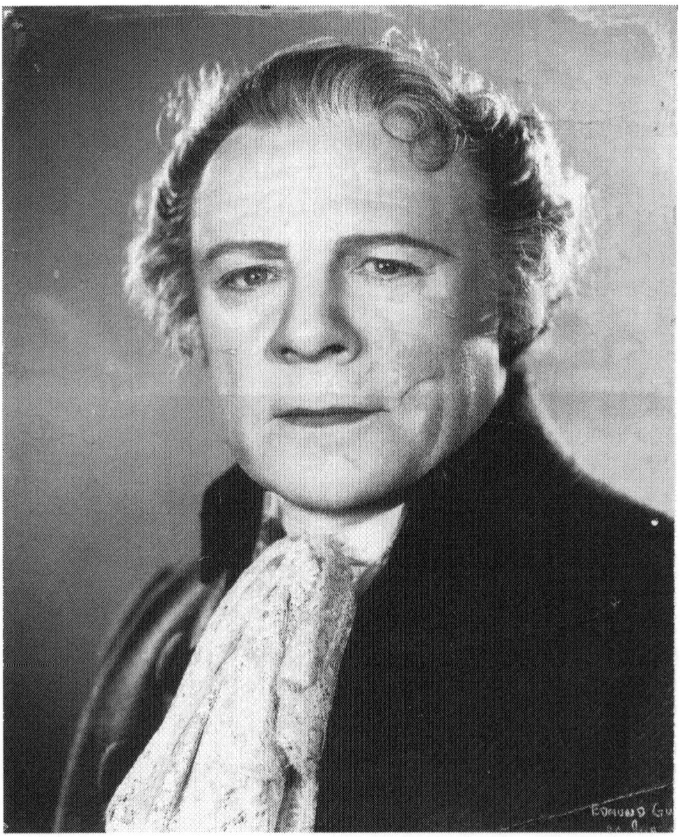

Edmund Gwenn in The Admiral's Secret

THE BALLOON GOES UP (1942)

Directed by Redd Davis (Easy Money, Say it With Diamonds, Discoveries)

Screenplay by Val Valentine

Produced by Edwin J Fancey

Starring: Ethel Revnell, Gracie West, Ronald Shiner, Donald Peers

Ethel and Gracie want to take part in the RAF camp concert but are not allowed in as they are not service personnel so they decide to join up and have to go for a medical. Later on they come across two German spies whom they expose and have arrested. They eventually do a comic turn at the concert.

Not very sophisticated humour even for the time (the Marx Brothers had been around for more than a decade employing clever wordplay and inventive sight gags) but it has its amusing moments.

Locations: no Merton Park locations, mainly studio.

Notes: This was producer Fancey's first film. A decade later he produced the Goons film Down Among the Z Men (1952). In1941 Fancey had gone to prison for stabbing his accountant in the groin. The accountant had to have a leg amputated as a result.

Comedian Ronald Shiner had been in films since 1934 and, incredibly, this was just one of nine films he made in 1942.

Donald Peers sings several songs in the film, but none of them appear to have been released on record. He later had a hit with his signature tune 'In a Shady Nook by a Babbling Brook' and continued having hit records into the 1970s.

SCHWEIK'S NEW ADVENTURES (aka It Started at Midnight – 1943)

Directed by Karel Lamac (Honeymoon, Hound of the Baskervilles)

Screenplay by Karel Lamac, Con West (characters based on the book The Good Soldier Schweik by Jaroslav Hasek)

Produced by Edward G Whiting

Starring: Lloyd Pearson, Maggie Rennie, Julien Mitchell, David Attenborough

An anti-Nazi satire set in Prague with some very black humour. When someone is being sent off to a concentration camp Schweik (Pearson) jokes, using the wartime fuel rationing line, 'Is your journey really necessary?' Similarly, when asked for his papers by a Nazi guard he says he never carries them as he is trying to save paper – 'don't you know there's a war on?'

He also explains the origins of the Nazi salute stemming from Hitler raising his arm when employed as a paper hanger.

The film is notable for featuring the nineteen year-old Richard Attenborough in his first credited screen role. He had been in Noel Coward's In Which We serve the previous year in an uncredited role as a stoker.

In this film he has a small speaking (and singing!) part as a railwayman who imparts secret information to some escaping prisoners with the ingenious ruse of singing instructions in Latin to the tune of O Sole Mio in the hope that the Nazis will not be able to distinguish Latin from Italian.

Locations: As far as can be established there was no outside shooting in the Merton Park area, just studio work.

Notes: The film included well-known character actor John Slater who later appeared in Merton Park film The Third Visitor (1951), and Barry Morse, later famous for his role as Lt Philip Gerard in long-running TV series The Fugitive. Lloyd Pearson also appeared in another Merton Park film, Hindle Wakes in 1952.

Jaroslav Hasek's original book The Good Soldier Schweik was set in the First World War and the screenwriters have simply used the subversive character of Schweik to undermine the authority and menace of the Second World War Nazi regime.

UP WITH THE LARK (1943)

Directed by Philip Brandon (Fallen Idol, Be Like the Kettle and Sing)

Written by Val Valentine, James Seymour

Produced by Edwin J Fancey

Starring: Ethel Revnell, Gracie West, Ivor Barnard

Ethel Revnell and Gracie West were a wartime music hall comedy duo who appeared in several films and on radio. Revnell was, at over six feet tall, a foot taller than West and they were known as 'The Long and the Short'. They were popular enough to have their own comic strips in Radio Fun comic, sometimes as 'Girls of the Giddy Patrol' and sometimes as 'Radio's Comical Cockney Kids.' They had appeared at nearby Wimbledon theatre just a couple of years previously (from September 1st 1941) in a revue entitled Looking Ahead, which was billed as 'a new riot of fun, mirth and melody'. The theatre programme included the advice: 'please remember your gas masks', and also gave details of nearby air raid shelters. In this film they are sacked from their jobs as telephone switchboard operators, become Land Girls and help foil a gang of black marketeers.

MY AIN FOLK (1945)

Directed by Germain Burger

Screenplay by Kathleen Butler

Produced by FW Baker

Starring: Moira Lister, Mabel Constanduros, Norman Prince, Herbert Cameron

Set in the Scottish Highlands, the story concerns a girl preventing a strike taking place at the factory where she works and she ends up organising a concert.

Locations: this film is not available on DVD and locations are not known though it is likely that Merton Park was only used for studio scenes.

Notes: Moira Lister later appeared in another Merton Park film, The Limping Man (1953) with Lloyd Bridges.

Nicolette Roeg also appeared in this film and was the older sister of director Nicolas Roeg (Don't Look Now, The Man Who Fell to Earth).

VOLGA VOLGA (1945)

Directed by Grigoriy Aleksandrov (British remake directed by Herbert Marshall)

Screenplay by Nikolay Erdman, Vladimir Nilsen

Produced by Igor Lopatonok

Starring: Igor Ilyinsky, Vladimir Volodin, Pavel Olenev

A strange one, this. Musical comedy Volga Volga was made in the USSR in 1938 and was reputedly Stalin's favourite film. It is said that he knew the dialogue off by heart and when he watched it he would quote the lines just before they were said or sung on screen, which must have been rather irritating for his guests.

A shortened version was made in 1945 with English voices (spoken and singing) dubbed on at Merton Park studios. One of those voices was that of celebrated actor Trevor Howard, who appeared that same year in his best-known role as Dr Alec Harvey in the classic British film Brief Encounter (1945).

TROUBLE AT TOWNSEND (1946)

Directed by Darrell Catling (The Adventures of Dusty Bates, The Cat Gang, Under the Frozen Falls)

Screenplay by Darrell Catling (based on the book by Malcolm Saville)

Produced by H Bruce Turner

Starring: Petula Clark, David Lees, Thea Wells, Peter Mullins

Set during the Second World War, the two children Mary and Mike Bishop (Clark and Lees) are sent to their uncle's farm while their mother spends time with their father who is home on leave.

On arriving at the farm they are given instructions by the uncle about how to behave in the countryside, closing gates, not lighting fires etc. Of course they immediately flout all the rules and get into trouble.

At one point in the film the thirteen year-old (though looking younger) Petula Clark sits at a piano and starts playing There's No Place Like Home. Her younger brother then says 'Ah, swing it sister!' and she goes into an uptempo piece to which he performs a spirited tap dance.

The film was apparently meant to teach children how to behave in the countryside and may have even had some government funding.

Locations: all the outside shooting was done in the area where Malcolm Saville lived in Hertfordshire, and Merton Park was used for the interior scenes.

Notes: this was Petula Clark's first film. She went on to appear in many others including Finian's Rainbow (1968) with Fred Astaire and Goodbye Mr Chips (1969) with Peter O'Toole.

The same year as this film Peter Mullins (who played the children's young cousin) appeared in Caravan (1946) with Stewart Granger.

The following year Darrell Catling directed The Adventures of Dusty Bates (1947), a film serial starring a sixteen year-old Anthony Newley as Bates in his first credited film role. His film The Cat Gang (1959) starred Francesca Annis – her first film.

FLYING WITH PRUDENCE (1946)

Directed by Cecil Musk (Circus Boy, Blow Your Own Trumpet)

Screenplay by Oswald Skilbeck

Produced by Frank A Hoare

Starring: Patricia Cutts, Derek Elphinstone

This was a dramatised instruction film for RAF air safety in peacetime. Dickie (Elphinstone) is a Flight Lieutenant in the RAF who meets Prudence (Cutts) at a dance and as he is due to fly her to India the next day starts to tell her how he misses the excitement of flying during the war. Prudence is unimpressed with the tales of his dangerous exploits and during the flight warns him several times of various dangers. At the end, when he kisses her goodbye she disappears only to reappear as a girl on a poster. A full description of the film's story can be found on the website of the Imperial War museum.

THE GLEN IS OURS (1946)

Directed by Henry Cass

Starring: Anthony Baird, Leo Hunter, Sheila Latimer, Edie Martin

A short drama about a Scottish glen that is due to be sold for development when a young soldier, returning from Burma, attempts to stop it by standing in the local elections. He is helped by his girlfriend, the daughter of a local councillor who is in favour of the development.

Mildly entertaining, and necessarily parochial, but interesting in its depiction of regional life and social attitudes of its time.

The film was made by the Central Office of Information and the music is by the London Symphony Orchestra. There appears to be no record of who wrote the script.

Locations: Some outside filming was done in Dunfermline but studio work was at Merton Park.

Notes: Edie Martin, who played the aging schoolmarm was later to appear in Ealing Comedies The Lavender Hill Mob, the Titfield Thunderbolt, the Ladykillers and the Man in the White Suit. She also had a small, uncredited, part in the Merton Park film Sparrows Can't Sing (1963), her last film.

Anthony Baird appeared in several minor roles in other Merton Park films such as the Counterfeit Plan (1957) and Devil Doll (1964).

CROFTERS (1946)

Directed by Ralph Keene

Made for the COI (Central Office of Information)

A short public information film about the life of crofters in Achriesgill in the remote Scottish highlands.

Made at the end of World War Two it is interesting as a social document of a way of life that had probably remained virtually unchanged for hundreds of years. The only concessions to modernity are some new houses being built and the post office van bringing not only mail, but also vital supplies of food and other essentials.

As most of the filming was done on location it is likely that Merton Park's main contribution was in sound and editing.

The music was performed by the London Symphony Orchestra conducted by John Hollingsworth.

NORTH-EAST CORNER (1946)

Directed by John Eldridge

Made for the COI (Central Office of Information)

An old fisherman compares his life with that of a modern one, and the film looks at the scenery and history of this part of Scotland. The film also includes a short stage performance by music hall star Alec Finlay at the Tivoli.

As above, Merton Park was probably only used for sound and editing facilities.

One of the two people providing the commentary was Cider With Rosie writer Laurie Lee.

THE CASE OF CHARLES PEACE (1949)

Directed by Norman Lee (Chamber of Horrors, Monkey's Paw)

Screenplay by Norman Lee, Doris Davison

Produced by John Argyle

Starring: Michael Martin Harvey, Chili Bouchier, Valentine Dyall

Based on the true story of Victorian burglar and murderer Charles Peace, this is part courtroom drama and part criminal career story of Peace shown in flashbacks.

An effective film carried by the idiosyncratic performance of Michael Martin Harvey in the lead role who alternates between a playful, puckish character and an unpleasant bully.

Locations: No Merton Park exteriors as far as can be seen; just studio work.

Notes: There is a local ghost story associated with this film. In his condemned cell Charles Peace is shown with a model of a cathedral that he had made while in prison. The actor who played him (Harvey) said that this was the actual model that the real-life Charles Peace had made in his condemned cell and when he (Harvey) touched it he felt a hand – 'hard, horny, and ice-cold' touching his. He also said he could feel Peace's presence especially when he was in the dock scenes.

THE FOOL AND THE PRINCESS (1949)

Directed by William C Hammond (Secret Tunnel, The Mysterious Poacher)

Screenplay by William C Hammond (based on the story by Stephen Spender)

Produced by Frank A Hoare

Starring: Bruce Lester, Lesley Brook, Irene Handl, Murray Matheson

Harry Granville (Lester) returns home after the war and finds it hard to adjust to civilian life. The story is narrated in the voice of his wife Kate (Brook). The film also uses flashbacks to show Harry meeting a young woman named Maura (Adina Mandlova) at a displaced persons camp in Germany just after the war and with whom he fell in love. He eventually returns to Europe to reconcile his feelings for her and to return to his wife.

In their book The British 'B' Film, Steve Chibnall and Brian McFarlane point out the similarities between this film and Brief Encounter – failed adultery, return to dull spouse, flashbacks, the use of classical music, undertones of homosexuality and the casting of Irene Handl who appeared in both films. They also mention the many positive reviews the film received in the press on release. Notes: the story by Stephen Spender was not published until 1958 when it was coupled with another novella, Engaged in Writing.

HA'PENNY BREEZE (1950)

Directed by Frank Worth (Accidents Don't Happen – documentary short)

Screenplay by Don Sharp, Frank Worth

Produced by Don Sharp, Darcy Conyers

Starring: Edwin Richfield, Don Sharp, Gwyneth Vaughan

David King (Richfield) and his Australian friend Johnny Craig (Sharp) go back to Suffolk fishing village Pin Mill after the war and find it has deteriorated badly from King's memories of it. They decide to revitalise the village by turning it into a yachting resort.

It is a gentle and low-key film deliberately made on a tiny budget to show what could be done without Hollywood dollars. In fact it became almost a collective when British Pathé advanced part of the budget and stipulated that everyone working on the film, from the producer downwards, would be paid a flat fee of £10 a week.

Locations: the film was entirely shot on location in the real-life coastal village of Pin Mill in Suffolk.

Notes: Michel Gough, who was to later star in several Merton Park films, plays a small, uncredited role. Don Sharp was to go on to direct The Face of Fu Manchu (1965) starring Christopher Lee, The Thirty Nine Steps (1978) starring Robert Powell, and Bear Island (1979) starring Donald Sutherland and Vanessa Redgrave.

THE GORBALS STORY (1950)

Directed by David MacKane

Screenplay by David MacKane (from the play by Robert MacLeish)

Produced by Ernest Gartside

Starring: Howard Connell, Marjorie Thomson, Betty Henderson, Russell Hunter

Something of a curiosity in Merton Park's output, this seems to be simply just the filming of a stage play by the Glasgow Unity Theatre, an amateur drama group with strong links to the Communist Party of Great Britain and the Left Book Club Theatre Guild.

It starts with successful artist Johnnie Martin (Hunter) looking back on his upbringing in the slums of Glasgow and the rest of the film is a flashback of those times until the end when he reflects on his good fortune in escaping the slums and making a successful career for himself.

It is really more of a melodrama with some overwrought acting and unashamed pathos. It does have its moments of wry humour and true drama but seems too parochial to be of wide interest.

The original play was first performed in 1946 at the Queen's Theatre, Gallowgate in Glasgow and went on to be performed a further 600 times over the next three years before this film version was made in 1950.

In 2015 the film was shown in the Gorbals for the first time since its original release as part of Glasgow's Southside Film Festival.

The Guardian described the film as a 'classic' and as a 'landmark' film which was unusual at the time for showing working class people as they really were and predating the 'kitchen sink' dramas of the late 1950s and 1960s.

Locations: There are one or two outside shots of Glasgow but the majority of the film is studio-based.

Notes: Lead actor Russell Hunter went on to have a lifelong career as a professional actor, appearing in TV series such as Callan and The Gaffer. Several other cast members also went on to professional acting work, mainly on TV.

MYSTERY JUNCTION (1951)

Directed by Michael McCarthy (Operation Amsterdam, The Accursed)

Screenplay by Michael McCarthy

Produced by William H Williams

Starring: Sydney Tafler, Barbara Murray, Martin Benson

A whodunnit set on a train with the feel of an Agatha Christie story. Crime writer Larry Gordon (Tafler) gets chatting to an elderly female fan on the train when they both hear a scream. On investigation they find a guard has been attacked and one of the police officers guarding a convict has disappeared. The remaining police officer orders everyone off the train at the next stop where they are all stranded in a waiting room due to a snowstorm.

Here, tensions build as the convict produces a gun and starts dictating events.

The film is quite stylishly done with some good performances from the leading actors but perhaps suffers from too much dialogue and difficult-to-follow plot twists. It has a surprise ending and finishes on a wry note with the elderly lady pulling down the train window blind revealing the words 'The end'. Notes: According to the IMDb website the film never got a cinema release in the USA but was shown on TV there in 1952.

THE DARK MAN (1951)

Directed by Jeffrey Dell (Carlton Browne of the F.O., It's Hard to be Good)

Screenplay by Jeffrey Dell

Produced by Julian Wintle

Starring: Edward Underdown, Maxwell Reed, Natasha Parry, William Hartnell

The 'Dark Man' (Reed) commits two murders within the first few minutes of this film but the second is witnessed by a young actress named Molly Lester (Parry). She reports it to the police and then gets romantically involved with one of the investigating officers, Detective Inspector Viner (Underdown).

It then becomes a simple cat and mouse game with the police pursuing the Dark Man until the eventual denouement at a bleak coastal area.

Despite the simplicity of the plot and the fact that we know 'whodunnit' from the outset this is an effective film noir thriller which creates atmosphere through well-chosen locations and believable characters.

Locations: There doesn't appear to have been any outside filming in the Merton Park area and the finale of the film was shot on location at Dungeness.

Notes: director Jeffrey Dell was at one time married to Jill Craigie who had directed documentary Out of Chaos (1944) at Merton Park and was later to marry Labour leader Michael Foot.

Julian Wintle went on to produce TVs the Avengers during its cult period from 1965–69 as well as films such as Tiger Bay starring Hayley Mills.

Maxwell Reed was to marry Joan Collins the following year (1952).

William Hartnell, who played the police superintendent, was of course to become the first Doctor Who – twelve years later, in 1963.

Although this film was made by Independent Artists Ltd (Julian Wintle's company) the opening credits show the famous Rank Organisation's man with a gong.

THE THIRD VISITOR (1951)

Directed by Maurice Elvey (Hindle Wakes, Stars in Your Eyes)

Screenplay by Gerald Anstruther (based on his play of the same title)

Produced by Ernest Gartside

Starring: Sonia Dresdel, Guy Middleton, Hubert Gregg, Karel Stepanek

A striking opening with a terrified woman manacled to a wall as a man threatens her with a gun. It then cuts to a disagreement between businessman Richard Carling (Stepanek) and New York Gangster James Oliver (John Slater) which ends with Carling apparently being murdered. His body is later discovered by his business partner.

The business partner, Jack Kurton (Gregg) and his wife are questioned by police as are a couple who are friends of theirs (played by Dresdel and Colin Gordon).

There are plenty of twists and turns in the plot and some witty dialogue as well as the curious, and rather creepy character of Hewson, played by Michael Martin Harvey.

When all the plot twists have finally been explained we find out what the seemingly disconnected opening sequence was all about.

An intriguing drama with a cast of good character actors, a sometimes witty script and one or two red herrings.

Locations: The film is mainly studio-bound so probably no location filming in the Merton Park area.

Notes: Maurice Elvey had directed two versions of Hindle Wakes (also known as Fanny Hawthorne) in 1918 and 1927, which are not to be confused with the 1952 version of Hindle Wakes made at Merton Park studios and directed by Arthur Crabtree. Elvey also directed The Great Game (1953) at Merton Park.

Colin Gordon appeared in several other Merton Park films and Michael Martin Harvey played the lead role in The Case of Charles Peace (1949) made at Merton Park.

Karel Stepanek had a leading role in another Merton Park film, The Frozen Dead (1966).

ASSASSIN FOR HIRE (1951)

Directed by Michael McCarthy (Operation Amsterdam, Mystery Junction)

Screenplay by Rex Rienits

Produced by Julian Wintle (This Sporting Life, Tiger Bay, Avengers TV series)

Starring: Sydney Tafler, Ronald Howard, Katherine Blake

A good, compact thriller that makes the most of Merton Park's budgetary limitations by sticking to a small number of mainly studio-bound sets.

Tafler plays Italian Antonio Riccardi, a criminal who masks his career as a hit man with a public face as a dealer of collectable postage stamps. His brother Giuseppe is a talented violinist whom Antonio is financing in an attempt to start him on a professional career.

The police suspect that Antonio is behind recent shootings and Detective Inspector Carson (Howard) tries to find a way of finally proving it.

At 64 minutes the film doesn't outstay its welcome and has a surprise ending that makes it a satisfying experience. Only one word of criticism is that Sydney Tafler does rather overdo the Italian accent.

Notes: This was the first feature film made by Anglo Amalgamated, the production company set up by Nat Cohen, Stuart Levy and Julian Wintle that had started as a distribution company.

Writer Rex Rienits also wrote screenplays for Merton Park productions Wide Boy and Noose For a Lady.

SING ALONG WITH ME (1952)

Directed by Peter Graham Scott (Night Creatures, Devil's Bait)

Screenplay by Peter Graham Scott, Dennis Vance

Produced by John Croydon

Starring: Donald Peers, Dodo Watts, Dennis Vance, Jill Clifford

Donald Peers plays grocer David Parry who wins a song writing contest on the radio and finds himself rather out of his depth in the showbiz world of London.

According to the website ringostrack.com the songs Donald Peers sings in the film include:

If you Smile at the Sun, Down at the Old Village Hall, Hoop-Diddle-I-De-Ra-Li-Ay, I Left My Heart in a Valley in Wales and Take My Heart.

Locations: at the time of writing this film is not available on DVD and locations are unknown.

Notes: online sources do not mention where this film was made, but in a 1995 interview (published in An Autobiography of British Cinema by Brian McFarlane) director Peter Graham Scott confirmed it was made at Merton Park. The Encyclopaedia of British Film, edited by Brian McFarlane says this film 'failed to launch the screen career of Donald Peers.' However, he had sung in a much earlier film at Merton Park, The Balloon Goes Up (1942) – see separate entry.

CROW HOLLOW (1952)

Directed by Michael McCarthy

Screenplay by Vivian Milroy (based on the novel by Dorothy Eden)

Produced by William H Williams

Starring: Donald Houston, Natasha Parry, Melissa Stribling, Patricia Owens

Young couple Robert and Anne (Houston and Parry) have only known each other a week but get married and plan to move to Crow Hollow, the family home of Robert, who is a doctor. Just before they do so, they visit Robert's dying aunt in hospital who warns Anne not to go there. The house is lived in by three of Robert's aunts and the attractive but capricious maid Willow (Owens) and a gardener.

Anne then has several unpleasant experiences – encountering a poisonous spider, eating poisoned soup, etc. which she believes may have been engineered by somebody, perhaps Willow – or perhaps one of the slightly dotty elderly aunts.

Is the house cursed or is somebody trying to kill her?

Locations: no Merton Park locations, mostly studio based.

Notes: Donald Houston had already been in some high-profile films; The Blue Lagoon with Jeans Simmons and A Run For Your Money with Alec Guinness (both 1949).

Natasha Parry went on to appear in Midnight Lace (1960) with Doris Day and Rex Harrison. She had already appeared in another Merton Park film, The Dark Man (1951).

Patricia Owens had appeared in a Merton Park film the year before this, Mystery Junction (1951).

HINDLE WAKES (1952)

Directed by Arthur Crabtree (Lilli Marlene, Horrors of the Black Museum)

Screenplay by John Baines (based on the play by Stanley Houghton)

Produced by William J Gell

Starring: Leslie Dwyer, Lisa Daniely, Brian Worth, Sandra Dorne, Bill Travers, Michael Medwin

Factory worker Jenny Hawthorn (Daniely) goes on a works outing to the seaside and begins a romantic relationship with the factory boss's son, Alan Jeffcote (Worth) who is already in a relationship with another woman of his own class.

She spends a further week away with him and enlists the help of her friend Mary to corroborate her story that she spent the time with her. Unfortunately Mary is killed in a sailing accident and the truth emerges to both sets of parents. The film then highlights the mores of the times (perhaps not that different in early 50s Northern Britain than it would have been in 1910 when the original play was written) when both sets of parents expect Alan to 'do the decent thing' and marry Jenny.

Jenny though surprises everyone with her independence of mind and makes her own decision about what will happen next.

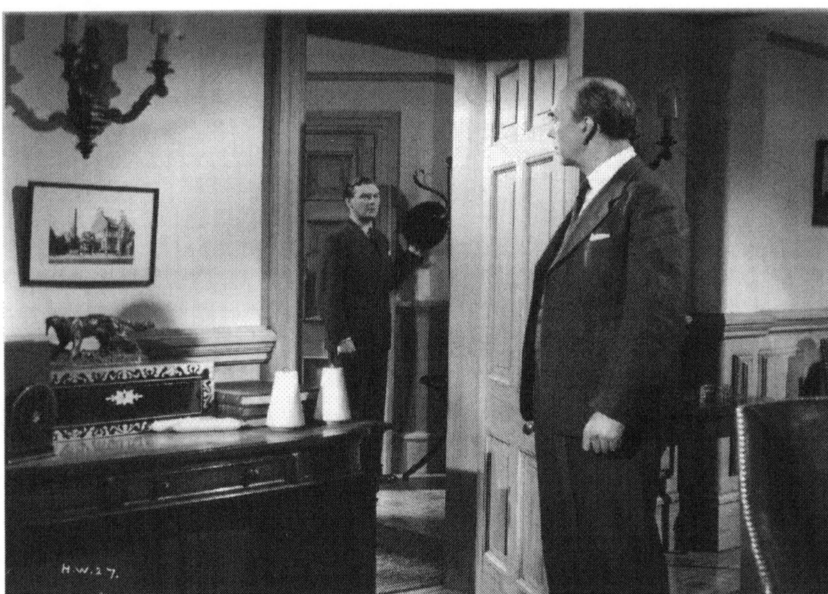

A good film, with strong performances but which perhaps betrays its origins as a morality tale written four decades earlier.

Locations: Although studio scenes were filmed at Merton Park there is location shooting in both Blackpool and Wales.

Notes: This was the fourth film version of the story. The first two, in 1918 and 1927, were silent, and the 1931 version a talkie. There was also a TV adaptation in 1976 by Jack Rosenthal, starring Rosalind Ayres and Roy Dotrice and directed by Sir Laurence Olivier and June Howson.

The film was released in the USA as Holiday Week.

Comic actress Rita Webb plays a small part in the film, her first.

WIDE BOY (1952)

Directed by Ken Hughes (Chitty Chitty Bang Bang, Casino Royale, Trials of Oscar Wilde)

Screenplay by Rex Rienits

Produced by Willliam H Williams

Starring: Sydney Tafler, Susan Shaw, Ronald Howard, Melissa Stribling

Almost a companion piece to Assassin For Hire from the previous year. It is by the same writer and also stars Sydney Tafler as a criminal and Ronald Howard as a police inspector. It even has the same actor (Ian Wallace) playing a cafe owner in both films.

Tafler is the eponymous 'wide boy' and, under pressure from his girlfriend (Shaw) to provide her with a better social life, moves from selling stolen nylons to blackmail.

Needless to say, this doesn't go to plan and before long the police are after wide boy Benny culminating in dramatic night time scenes at a railway bridge.

Dark and atmospheric, the film works well with images of a lost London of gas lit alleyways, minimal road traffic, steam trains and bobbies on the beat.

Locations: No outside filming in the Merton Park area.

Notes: This was director Ken Hughes' first feature film The subtitle shown on posters was rather misleading. It read 'Her lust for money stopped at nothing – even murder!', which made it sound as though there is a female murderer in the film, which was not the case.

Glyn Houston, later to appear in other Merton Park productions, had a small part in this film as a barman.

GHOST SHIP (1952)

Directed and produced by Vernon Sewell

Screenplay by Vernon Sewell

Starring: Dermot Walsh, Hazel Court

A young couple buy a yacht and are warned that it is haunted. Although the husband (Walsh) initially dismisses the notion the couple start to experience strange happenings aboard the ship. They bring in a psychic and a medium and eventually get to the bottom of the mystery.

Quite a good little thriller though it takes some time to get going due to some lengthy exposition in the first twenty minutes.

Atmospheric and given some added exoticism with the setting at sea and a fair bit of location filming.

Locations: Some location work done at Brighton, but studio work is Merton Park.

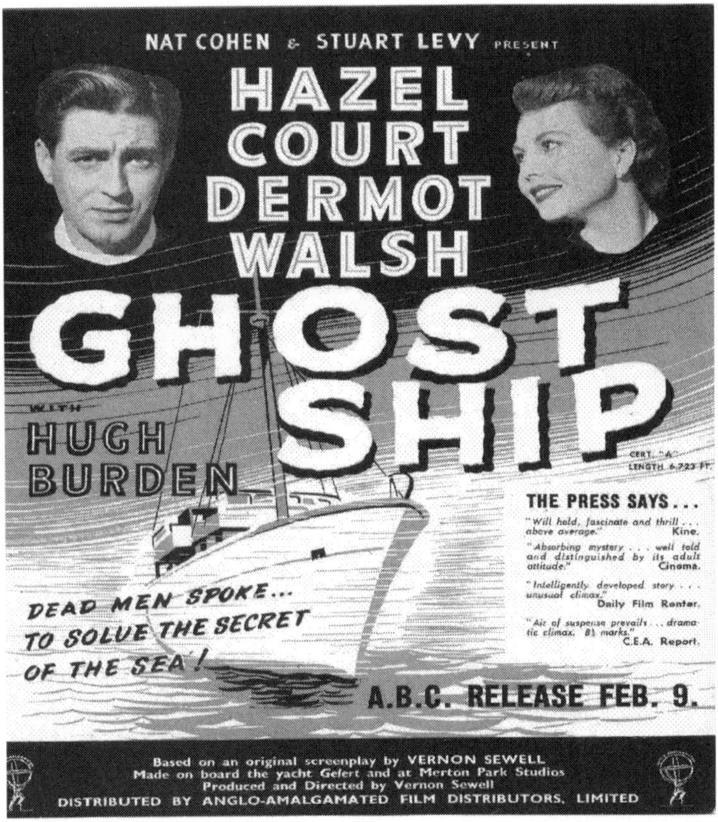

Notes: The leading couple, Walsh and Court were married in real life and made another film at Merton Park (Counterspy) the following year – 1953.

The ship used in the film, Gelert, belonged to director Vernon Sewell.

A young Ian Carmichael plays a small part in the film as a drunk at the on-board party, adding a bit of comic relief.

FLOATING DUTCHMAN (1952)

Directed by Vernon Sewell (Ghost ship, Dangerous Voyage, Silver Fleet)

Screenplay by Vernon Sewell (based on the novel by Nicholas Bentley)

Produced by William H Williams

Starring: Dermot Walsh, Sydney Tafler, Mary Germaine

A dead body is found in the Thames which turns out to be that of a Dutch diamond smuggler. Dermot Walsh plays undercover policeman Alexander James, who manages to infiltrate the smuggling gang which is led by Victor Skinner (Tafler), who also runs a nightclub.

Some good characterization by several of the cast even though the film overall may not have aged as well as some of Merton Park's others.

Notes: writer Nicholas Bentley has a small acting part in the film. He was also a very successful book illustrator and supplied drawings for TS Eliot's Old Possum's Book of Practical Cats (among others).

Director Vernon Sewell's yacht, Gelert, also appears in this film as it had in the Merton Park productions Ghost Ship and Dangerous Voyage.

When shown on US TV the film was retitled Clue For A Corpse.

MURDER AT SCOTLAND YARD (1952)

Directed by Victor M Gover (King of the Underworld, Strangler's Morgue)

Screenplay by John Gilling

Produced by Gilbert Church

Starring: Patrick Barr, Tod Slaughter, Tucker McGuire

Criminal Terence Reilly (Slaughter) has escaped from prison and stolen some diamonds and has also committed several murders. He is being pursued by private detective Inspector Morley (Barr). This was a sequel to the 1952 film King of the Underworld, with the same main cast members, but which had been shot at Bushey studios. There was also a third film in this series, Murder at the Grange, also made at Bushey studios in 1952 but which was much shorter, at just 31 minutes.

Locations: this film is not available on DVD and information about it is scant so locations are unknown. Notes: Tod Slaughter had been a stage actor since 1905and went into films in 1934, specialising in over-the-top villains in Victorian melodramas.

DEATH GOES TO SCHOOL (1953)

Directed by Stephen Clarkson

Screenplay by Stephen Clarkson and Maisie Sharman (based on a novel by Maisie Sharman writing as Stratford Davis)

Produced by Victor Hanbury

Starring: Gordon Jackson, Pamela Alan, Barbara Murray, Sam Kydd

A female schoolteacher is murdered in the grounds of a girls' school and Detective Inspector Campbell (Jackson) and his sidekick (Kydd) arrive to question the suspects – mainly the other teachers.

The film is slowed down rather by the painstaking questioning of each suspect one by one and by the frequent flashbacks but is kept watchable by the strong performances of the main cast members, particularly Jackson, and some witty lines. When Jackson asks one of the suspects about a detective story she has been reading she tells him that the crime is solved by an amateur detective. 'Naturally' responds Jackson drily.

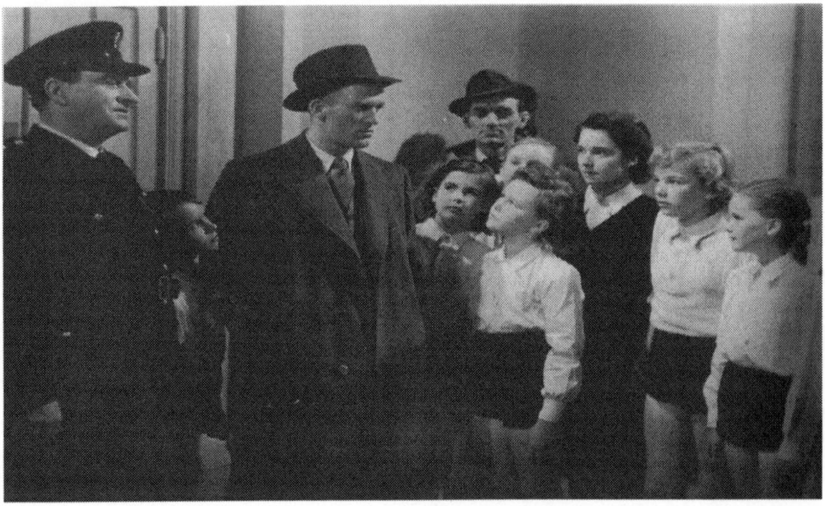

Locations: Some outside filming in several streets in Merton Park (e.g. Sheridan and Mostyn Roads).

Notes: When the teacher is asked what book she had been reading at the time of the murder she replies 'Death in Seven Hours'. This was the title of the book by Maisie Sharman (as Stratford Davis) on which this film was based. Maisie Sharman adopted the male pseudonym for her thriller writing as she thought it would give her more chance of being published.

THE GREAT GAME (1953)

Directed by Maurice Elvey (Stars in Your Eyes, Hindle Wakes)

Screenplay by Wolfgang Wilhelm (based on a play by Basil Thomas)

Produced by David Dent

Starring: James Hayter, Thora Hird, Diana Dors, Glyn Houston

The chairman of Burnville United football club, Joe Lawson (Hayter), tries to poach player Ned Rutter (Houston) from another team and he just happens to be engaged to one of his office staff. The underhand tactics result in Lawson losing his job as chairman and along the way being lectured by Rutter's fiancée about the ethics involved and the poor treatment of players.

Thora Hird and Diana Dors play supporting roles as office staff at the club and have their own subplots to keep the film interesting. It also includes John Laurie (Frazer in Dad's Army) in a small, but amusing role as one of Burnville United's staff.

Locations: No outside filming in Merton Park area; all location shooting done at Griffin Park, home of Brentford FC.

Notes: Tommy Lawton, player/manager at Brentford FC, makes a cameo appearance in the film.

Director Maurice Elvey had been directing films for forty years before this, starting in 1913 in the silent film era and directing the silent version of Hindle Wakes in 1927 – not to be confused with the 1952 version which was made at Merton Park.

NOOSE FOR A LADY (1953)

Directed by Wolf Rilla (Children of the Damned, Strange Affection)

Screenplay by Rex Rienits (based on novel by Gerald Verner)

Produced by Victor Hanbury

Starring: Dennis Price, Rona Anderson, Ronald Howard, Pamela Alan

The film starts with a woman, Margaret Allan (Pamela Alan), in court receiving the death sentence for the murder of her husband. Her cousin Simon (Price) turns up at the family home and starts making enquiries, virtually turning detective in his pursuit of the truth which he tries to uncover in the seven days left until Margaret's hanging.

It almost becomes like an Agatha Christie murder mystery, even culminating in a scene where all the suspects are gathered in one room with Price revealing, Poirot-style, the identity of the murderer.

It's a good film with a variety of 'characters' to keep it interesting and keeps the viewer guessing till the end.

Locations: No Merton Park location filming, in fact, very little outside shooting at all.

Notes: The cast includes Esma Cannon, a character actress who appeared in several Carry On films and numerous TV series.

It also includes Ian Wallace (who had appeared in other Merton Park productions such as Wide Boy and Assassin For Hire) and who was in the 1985 film Plenty with Meryl Streep. In addition to his acting career he was also a professional opera singer and was awarded an OBE.

STREET OF SHADOWS (aka Shadow Man – 1953)

Directed by Richard Vernon (producer of the Life & Death of Colonel Blimp, Kiss the Blood Off My Hands)

Screenplay by Richard Vernon (based on the novel The Creaking Chair by Laurence Meynell)

Produced by William H Williams

Starring: Cesar Romero, Kay Kendall, Victor Maddern, Simone Silva

An effective film noir that recreates the seedy side of post-war Soho. Romero plays Luigi, the owner of a club and Victor Maddern plays the part of 'Limpy' his partially disabled factotum.

Romero has a brief affair with Barbara Gale (Kendall) whose husband seems more interested in gambling and girls other than her. In the meantime, Luigi's ex-girlfriend Angele (Silva) is found dead in his flat and the police are called. Luigi goes into hiding until the police find out who did it.

Very atmospheric with some haunting soundtrack music including a plaintive harmonica. The opening has a very American feel to it even though it was filmed on the streets of Soho.

Victor Maddern is excellent as 'Limpy', turning in a great character performance. Romero has a big screen presence and adds a bit of exoticism as does Simone Silva. Kay Kendall is something of an English rose amongst the thorns of Soho nightlife and conveys her vulnerability well.

Locations: most of the outside filming seems to have been done in central London, so no Merton Park locations, just studio work.

Notes: The film was released in the USA as Shadow Man.

Cesar Romero appeared in many other films but is best-known for his portrayal of The Joker in the original Batman TV series in the 1960s. He had also been well-known to a previous generation in the 1940s as the Cisco Kid.

Kay Kendall died at the tragically early age of 32 in 1959. She had been married to Rex Harrison.

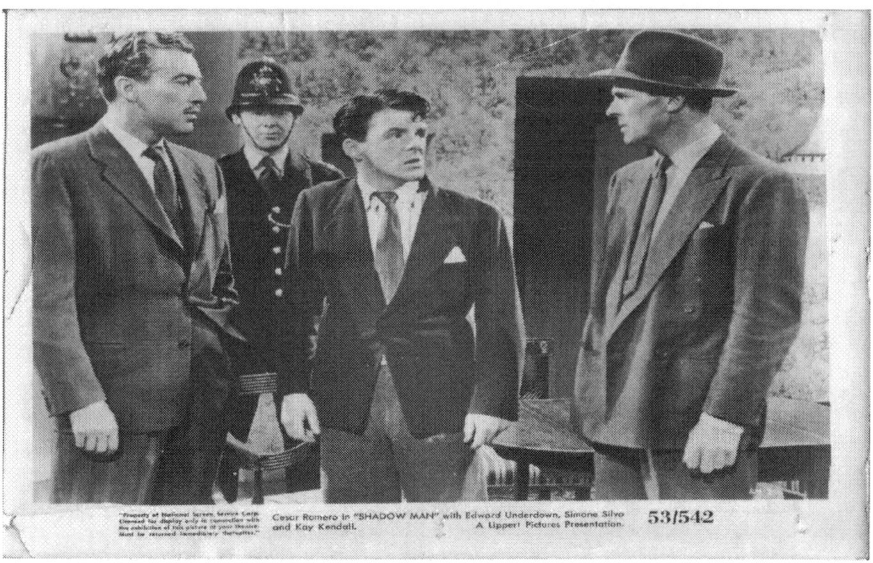

OPERATION MALAYA (aka Terror in the Jungle – 1953)

Directed by David MacDonald (Devil Girl From Mars, The Brothers)

Screenplay by David MacDonald, John Croydon

Produced by Herman Cohen

Starring: John Humphrey, John Slater, Chips Rafferty

This was a hybrid film, partly documentary footage and partly re-enactments. British troops are tracking down Communists who have killed the owner of a rubber plantation.

Locations: film not available on DVD but assumed that studio re-enactments filmed at Merton Park.

Notes: director David MacDonald approached the Colonial Office for funding, but they refused on the grounds that this was a commercial film, so he obtained funding from Sir Alex Korda.

Herman Cohen went on to produce other films at Merton Park including Horrors of the Black Museum (1959) and Konga (1961).

John Slater had appeared in a previous Merton Park film, The Third Visitor (1951).

THE LIMPING MAN (1953)

Directed by Cy Endfield (Zulu, Hell Drivers, Sands of the Kalahari) as Charles de Lautour

Screenplay by Ian Stuart Black, Reginald Long (based on the novel Death on the Tideway by Anthony Verney)

Produced by Donald Ginsberg

Starring: Lloyd Bridges, Moira Lister, Alan Wheatley, Leslie Phillips, Helene Cordet

American ex-soldier Franklin Prior (Bridges) comes back to England after World War Two to rekindle a romance with Pauline French (Lister) but as he is walking across the tarmac after his plane touches down the man next to him is shot by a sniper. Prior then finds that Pauline had a connection with the dead man.

Two Scotland Yard detectives investigate and are led to the victim's ex-wife, an actress named Helene Castle (Cordet) who is working as a singer and stage magician's assistant.

It is an interesting and engrossing film with additional atmosphere provided by some of the theatrical performances of Castle and others as well as some characterful location filming at a Thameside pub.

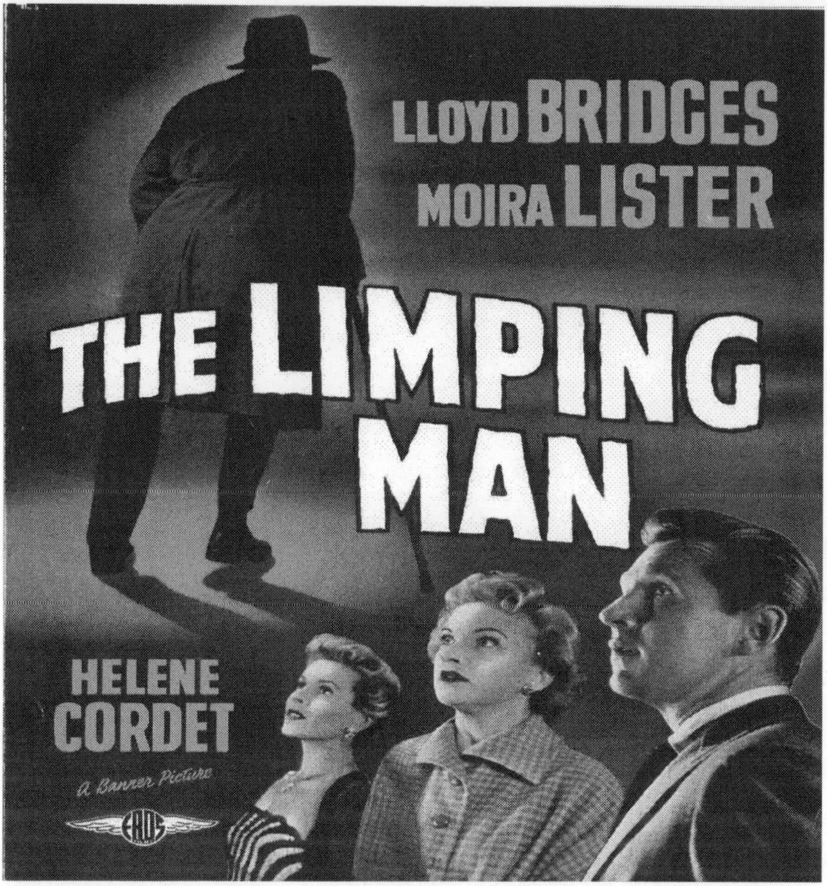

Unfortunately the film is rather let down by an unsatisfactory surprise ending, but what has preceded it is very watchable.

Locations: No outside filming in the Merton Park area but some interesting scenes on and around the Thames.

Notes: A young Lionel Blair has a dance routine in one of the scenes at the theatre where he dances on giant piano keys.

Leslie Philips plays the junior of the two investigating detectives and even at this early stage of his career is cast as a leering ladies' man.

Two actresses who were later to become very famous had small parts in the film, Rachel Roberts as a barmaid and Jean Marsh as the landlady's daughter (her screen debut). Another actor to make his screen debut in the film was Stephen Boyd in an uncredited role as an air traveller. By the end of the decade he was starring in Ben Hur.

Helene Cordet sings a couple of songs in the theatre scenes of the film, and one of them, Hey Presto was co-written by David Croft, later to write sitcoms such as Dad's Army, Are You Being Served, Hi-De-Hi and 'allo 'allo.

COUNTERSPY (aka Undercover Agent – 1953)

Directed by Vernon Sewell (Radio Cab Murder, Ghost Ship)

Screenplay by Guy Elmes, Gaston Lazare (based on the short story Criss Cross Code by Julian Symons)

Produced by William H Williams

Starring: Dermot Walsh, Hazel Court, Hermione Baddeley, Ben Travers

Another Merton Park film starring the real-life husband and wife Dermot Walsh and Hazel Court as husband and wife, though in this film Court has a much smaller part than Walsh.

It's a comedy thriller in which Walsh plays a mild-mannered auditor who gets caught up in espionage involving some secret plans that are being chased both by criminals and by British government agents.

It works well both as a thriller and as a comedy, combining some fast-paced action with excellent character acting – in particular, Hermione Baddeley as a matriarchal fortune teller and Alexander Gauge as a would-be gentlemanly villain.

Locations: No outside filming in Merton Park area as far as can be established.

Notes: The film was titled Undercover Agent in the US and the poster showed the second screenwriter not as Gaston Lazare but as Michael Le Fevre. It also says 'A Herman Cohen presentation' (Cohen wrote and produced the Merton Park films Horrors of the Black Museum, Headless Ghost and Konga).

Alexander Gauge was well-known in the 1950s as Friar Tuck in the Robin Hood TV series.

Ben Travers was the leading man in Born Free (1966).

DANGEROUS VOYAGE (aka Terror Ship – 1954)

Directed by Vernon Sewell (Ghost Ship, Floating Dutchman)

Screenplay by Vernon Sewell, Julia Ward

Produced by William H Williams

Starring: William Lundigan, Naomi Chance, Vincent Ball

A young couple find a ship adrift at sea with two men on board but by the time they help bring it to shore the two men have disappeared. A visiting American takes an interest in the ship and together the three of them set out to discover the mystery behind it.

This involves travelling to France and getting into various scrapes including having a gun fired at them, and an amusing encounter with gendarmes who misinterpret their attempts to explain themselves.

They eventually get to the bottom of it and the film has a spectacular and dramatic ending that goes beyond the usual budgetary limitations of Merton Park films.

Locations: quite a lot of outside filming at Shoreham-by-Sea and Trouville in France, but none in the Merton Park area.

Notes: director Vernon Sewell's ship, the Gelert, was used in the film and even kept its name! Sewell had also used the ship in the Merton Park film Ghost Ship a couple of years earlier.

The film was released in the USA with the title Terror Ship and the poster promised 'Excitement that rocks the screen'.

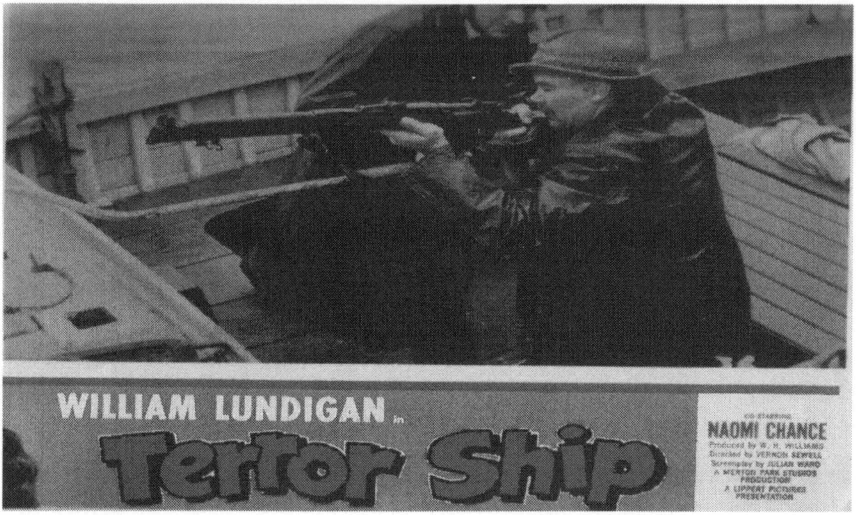

THE BRAIN MACHINE (1954)

Directed by Ken Hughes (Trials of Oscar Wilde, Casino Royale, Chitty Chitty Bang Bang)

Screenplay by Ken Hughes

Produced by Alec C Snowden

Starring: Patrick Barr, Elizabeth Allan, Maxwell Reed

A strange one this, as it looks from the posters and from the opening of the film to be a sci-fi story but after some initial focussing on an EEG machine and its use on drug smuggler Frank Smith (Maxwell Reed) it settles down to be a fairly straightforward crime thriller in the vein of one of Merton Park's Edgar Wallace or Scotland Yard films. In fact, the police inspector in this film is played by Russell Napier who played Inspector Duggan in over a dozen of the Scotland Yard films.

Some good performances from the cast and interesting to see a woman (Elizabeth Allan as Dr Philippa Roberts) being portrayed as assertive and liberated in a film of this vintage.

Much was made in the publicity material of the newness of the 'brain machine' technology and the fascination which the viewing public would have for it, but it had been in development for decades before this, though the first International EEG congress was held in 1953 just before this film was made.

Locations: No Merton Park locations.

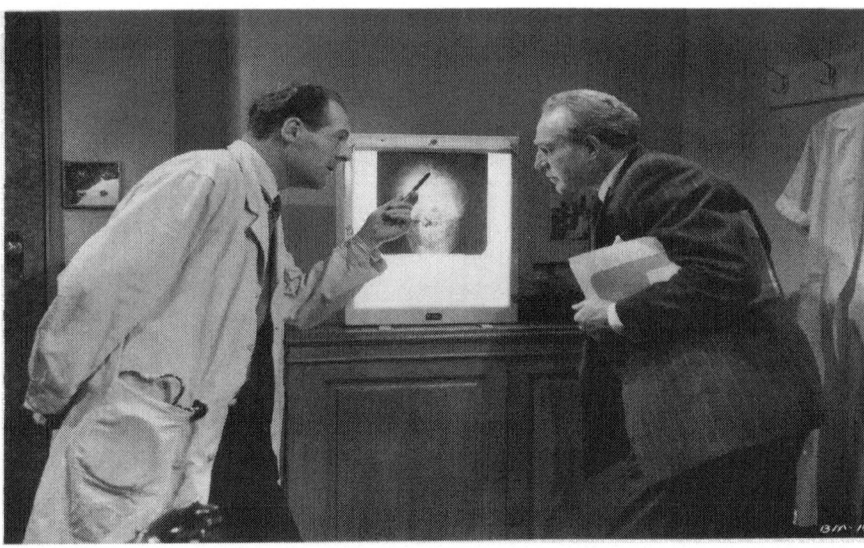

Notes: It has been suggested that the 'brain machine' (EEG) element was added to the film to cash in on other sci-fi style films of the time such as the Quatermass Experiment. Maxwell Reed was Joan Collins' first husband. He had also appeared in an earlier Merton Park film, The Dark Man (1951) alongside William Hartnell (the first Doctor Who) and Barbara Murray.

THE WAY OUT (aka Dial 999 – 1955)

Directed by Montgomery Tully (Query, Third Alibi)

Screenplay by Montgomery Tully and Bruce Graeme (based on his novel The Way Out)

Produced by Alec C Snowden

Starring: Gene Nelson, Mona Freeman, John Bentley, Michael Goodliffe)

Greg Carradine (Nelson) comes home one night and tells his wife that he has been wrongly accused of killing a man and that he needs her assistance to escape the police.

The wife (Freeman), and Carradine's brother (Goodliffe) go to extraordinary lengths to protect Greg but begin to have their doubts about his innocence of the crime. With the police in pursuit and a supporting cast of solid actors such as Sydney Tafler playing an underworld fixer it is an engaging and gripping film, and with quite a lot of location filming it becomes bigger than some of Merton Park's more studio-bound crime thrillers.

Locations: quite a lot of location shooting, some of which appears to be in the Merton Park/Wimbledon area.

Bruce Graeme, the writer on whose book the screenplay was based, was one of the founding members of the Crime Writer's Association of Britain.

Montgomery Tully also directed several other films at Merton Park, including Man With a Gun, Female Fiends (aka Strange Awakening), and the Electronic Monster (all 1958).

TIMESLIP (aka The Atomic Man – 1955)

Directed by Ken Hughes (Chitty Chitty Bang Bang, Casino Royale, Cromwell)

Screenplay by Charles Eric Maine

Produced by Alec C Snowden

Starring: Gene Nelson, Faith Domergue, Peter Arne

An atomic scientist is found in a river after having been shot. He dies in hospital, but then comes back to life, though his mind is now out of sync with his body by seven and a half seconds.

Things are further complicated by the fact that the scientist, or someone masquerading as him, continues to work in his laboratory. Who is the imposter?

The police – and the press – intend to find out.

Both the leading man (Nelson) and leading lady (Domergue) are American and so add a bit of international glamour to this film. Nelson's wise-cracking Mike Delaney character, a science journalist, also adds some razzmatazz that helps give the film some gloss and enhance what is mainly a studio-bound film.

All in all it's very watchable and has some interesting plot twists and good character acting.

Like many of Merton Park's sci-fi/horror films of the 1950s and 1960s it also has some great poster artwork. The artwork for this is almost psychedelic and worth buying the DVD for this alone!

Locations: According to IMDb there was some location filming done in Wimbledon.

Notes: Charles Hawtrey (of 'Carry On' fame) has a scene-stealing comedy role as 'the office boy' – even though he was 41 years old at the time!

Charles Eric Maine, who wrote the screenplay, later based a novel on the story, entitled The Isotope Man (published 1959). He also wrote the novel Escapement (1956) on which the Merton Park film Electronic Monster (1958) was based, and for which he also wrote the screenplay.

The film was released in the USA as The Atomic Man and was on a double bill with Invasion of the Body Snatchers.

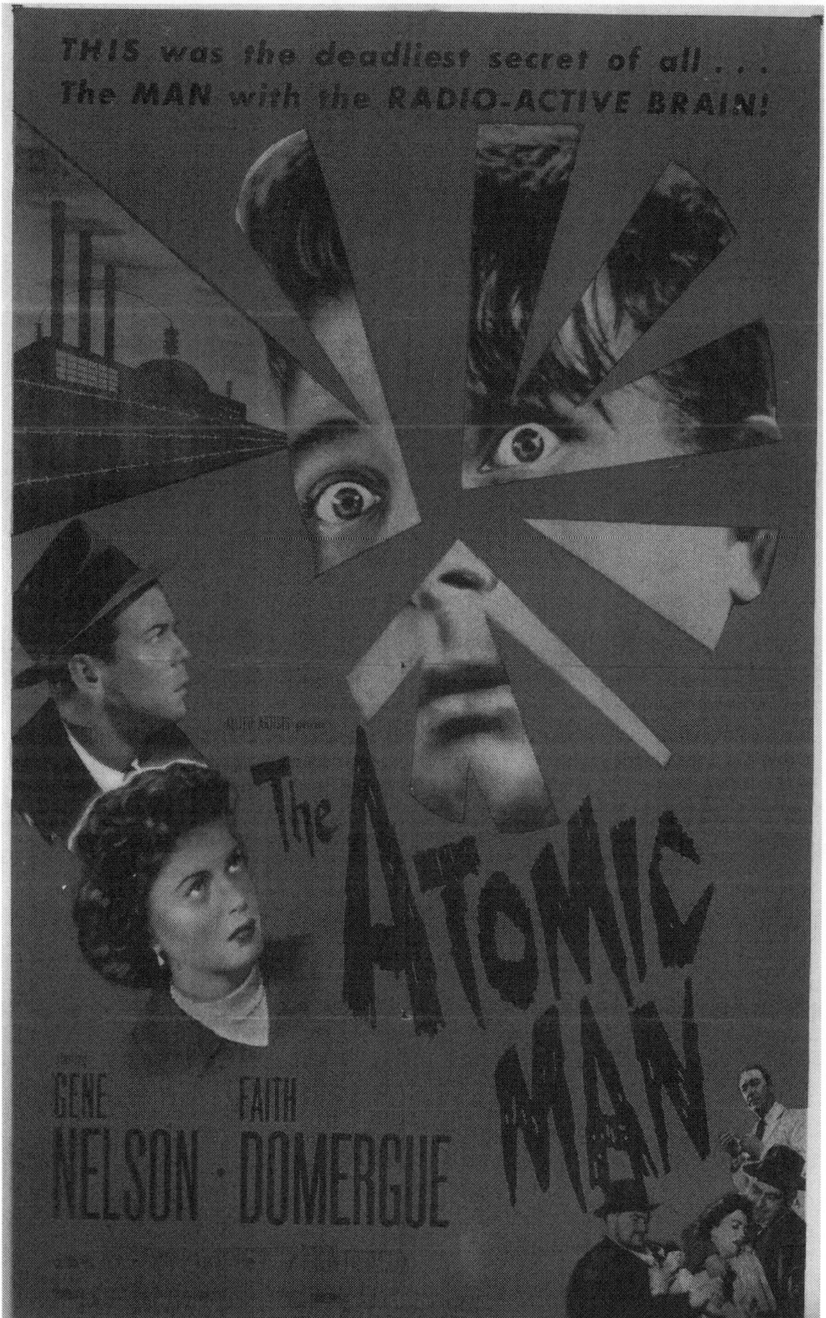
THIS was the deadliest secret of all . . .
The MAN with the RADIO-ACTIVE BRAIN!
The ATOMIC MAN
GENE NELSON · FAITH DOMERGUE

CONFESSION (aka The Deadliest Sin – 1955)

Directed by Ken Hughes (Chitty Chitty Bang Bang, Casino Royale, Cromwell)

Screenplay by Ken Hughes (based on the play by Don Martin)

Produced by Alec C Snowden

Starring: Sydney Chaplin, Audrey Dalton, Jefferson Clifford

The film starts with a man confessing to a priest that he has committed a murder and due to the 'sacramental seal' the priest is obliged to keep quiet about it.

Then the story proper starts with a flashback and we see Mike Nelson (Chaplin) coming back to his family home in England after a long business trip to the USA. He has acquired a full American accent and this therefore gives Merton Park a reason again to employ an American actor to add to a film's international appeal.

We gradually find out that Mike has been involved in some shady deals in the US and has people after him looking for revenge. This he tries to keep from his sister (Dalton) and her boyfriend, but somehow they get mixed up in the subterfuge with deadly results.

A good film with a plot that is not a million miles from Hitchcock's I Confess (1953), but intriguing and gripping enough in its own right with a very dramatic ending.

The publicity material for the film suggested newspaper competitions in which readers could name an eighth sin to add to the seven deadly sins; and it also put forward the idea of cinemas interviewing the 'head of your local homicide squad' to discuss the latest methods of scientific detection – tying it in of course with the story of this film!

Locations: no known Merton Park outside locations, just studio.

Notes: Sydney Chaplin was the son of Charlie Chaplin and in the same year made two other films, Abdullah's Harem with Kay Kendall and Land of the Pharaohs with Jack Hawkins and Joan Collins.

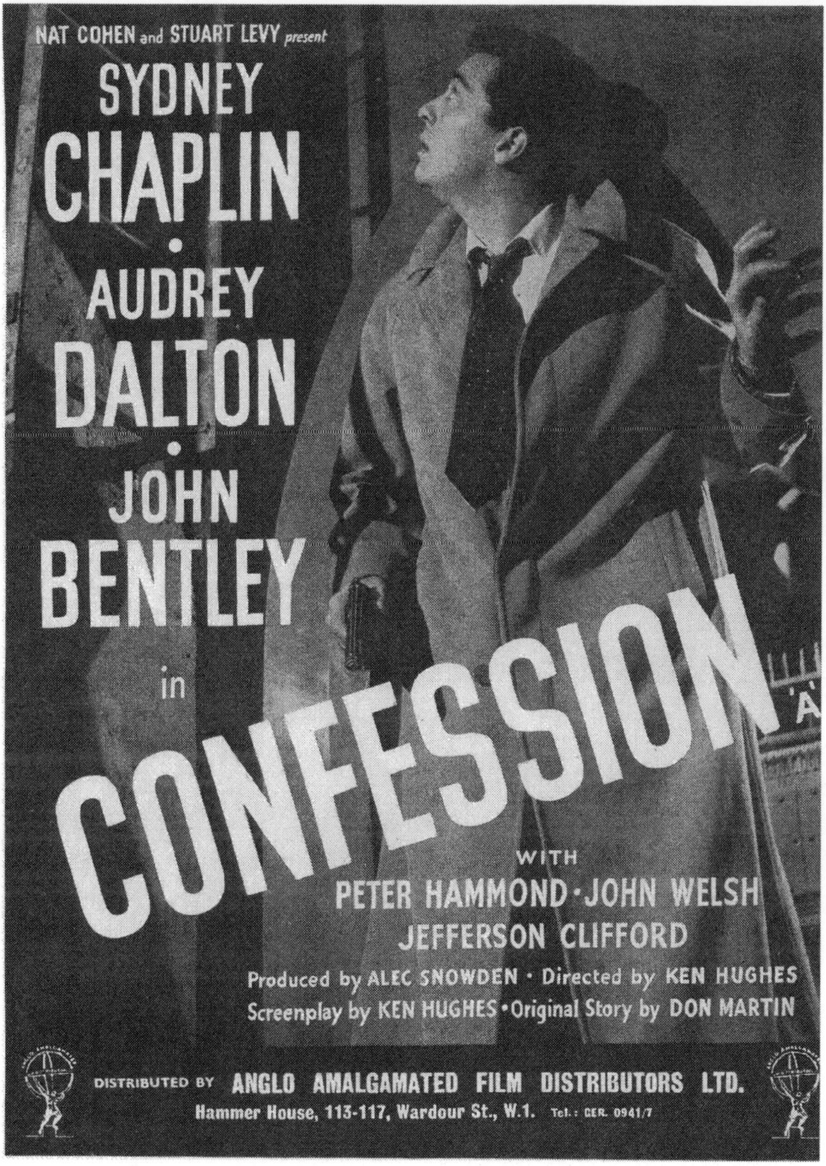
NAT COHEN and STUART LEVY present
SYDNEY CHAPLIN
AUDREY DALTON
JOHN BENTLEY
in
CONFESSION
'A'
WITH
PETER HAMMOND · JOHN WELSH
JEFFERSON CLIFFORD
Produced by ALEC SNOWDEN · Directed by KEN HUGHES
Screenplay by KEN HUGHES · Original Story by DON MARTIN
DISTRIBUTED BY ANGLO AMALGAMATED FILM DISTRIBUTORS LTD.
Hammer House, 113-117, Wardour St., W.1. Tel.: GER. 0941/7

LITTLE RED MONKEY (aka Case of the Red Monkey – 1955)

Directed by Ken Hughes (Casino Royale, Chitty Chitty Bang Bang, Cromwell)

Screenplay by Ken Hughes and James Eastwood (based on a story by Eric Maschwitz)

Produced by Alec C Snowden

Starring: Richard Conte, Rona Anderson, Russell Napier

A cold war spy drama about the mysterious murders of several nuclear scientists in the UK and the attempts of the authorities and the police to avert the murder of a visiting Russian scientist.

The common thread to the murders is the presence of the titular 'little red monkey'.

A good enough thriller for its time with some strong performances from the main cast though perhaps the plot is a little thin to be spread over 71 minutes.

Before this film was released there had been a six-part TV series entitled The Little Red Monkey starring Honor Blackman and Donald Houston and aired in January and February 1953 on the BBC. There was even a hit record of the theme tune, performed by Frank Chacksfield's Tunesmiths and other versions including one by comedian Jimmy Edwards. The film was released in the USA (titled Case of the Red Monkey) and across Europe and did very well. According to the book British 'B' Film by Steve Chibnall and Brian McFarlane, this film and another 1955 Merton Park production, Confession, were breakthrough films for Anglo-Amalgamated who made a lot of films at Merton Park from 1951 onwards. The success of these two it seems allowed the company to spend more on future productions and increase the quality of its films.

American leading man Richard Conte helped to add a bit of glamour and international appeal, being already established as a film actor.

Russell Napier, who had appeared in more than a dozen of Merton Park's Scotland Yard series episodes as a police inspector also appeared in this film in that role.

The American publicity material for the film suggested that cinemas print a series of monkey handprints on the pavements leading to the cinemas where it was showing. One of the poster slogans was 'A phantom killer strikes again and again … man, woman, or beast?'

Notes: Richard Conte went on to play Barzini in the Godfather (1972). Rona Anderson was in The Prime of Miss Jean Brodie in 1969 alongside Maggie Smith and Gordon Jackson, whom she had married in 1951.

This was the film debut (in a small, uncredited part) of Ed Devereaux, who later became well-known for his role in the TV series Skippy the Bush Kangaroo.

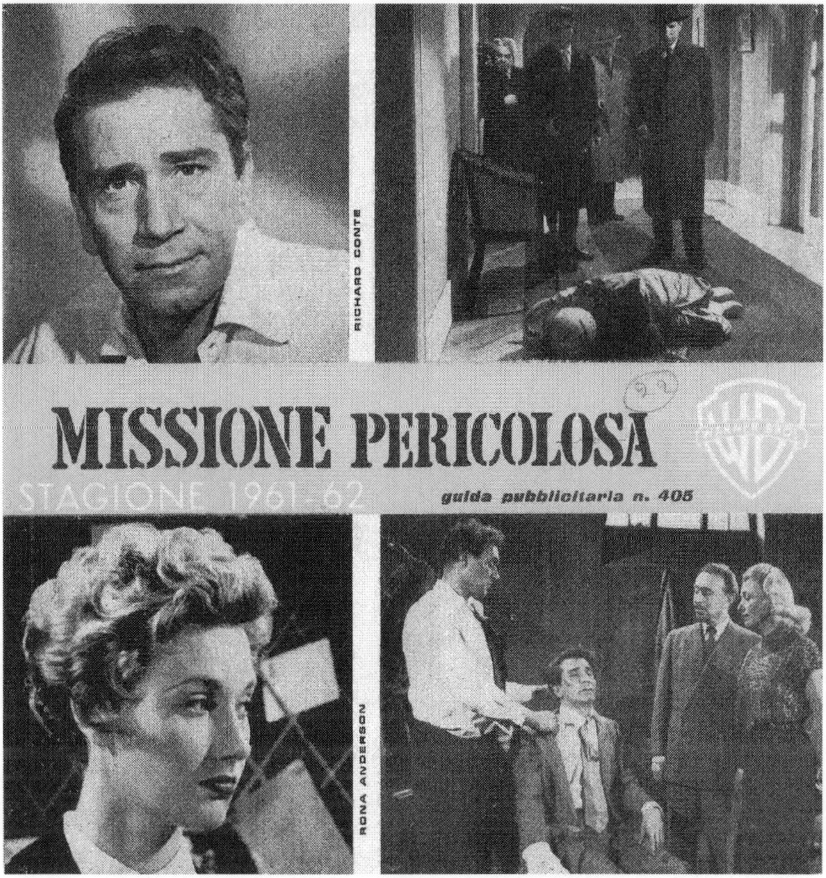

Little Red Monkey (Italian press book)

THE NARROWING CIRCLE (1956)

Directed by Charles Saunders (A Time to Kill, The Red Dress)

Screenplay by Doreen Montgomery (based on the book by Julian Symons)

Produced by Frank Bevis

Starring: Paul Carpenter, Hazel Court, Russell Napier, Trevor Reid

Crime writer Dave Nelson (Carpenter) is accused of murdering colleague Bill Strayte (Ferdy Mayne) who has beaten him to promotion at the magazine where they both work.

Nelson has an alibi for the time of the murder but mysteriously, the people who could have confirmed it are either missing or deny ever seeing him.

As the plot unfolds the body count rises and Nelson is implicated each time. The investigating detective, Inspector 'Dumb' Crambo (Reid) has a nice line in supercilious remarks and an ingratiating manner and helps keep up the entertainment level.

For once, Russell Napier is not playing the detective, but the magazine editor. Nelson's female colleague Rosemary Speed (Court) is the only one who believes Nelson's story and provides the love interest.

It's an entertaining film and has some good performances by an ever-reliable cast, but it must be said that it contains some of the most unconvincing fight scenes even for a film of this vintage.

Notes: James Booth plays a small, uncredited part in the film and, a few years later, took a lead part in Merton Park film Sparrows Can't Sing (1963).

The film's credits do not say where the film was made, but many of the crew had worked on other Merton Park films and leading actors such as Russell Napier and Hazel Court were Merton Park regulars so it seems safe to assume it was made at Merton Park.

Julian Symons, writer of the book on which the film was based, also wrote the novel Criss Cross Code on which Merton Park film Counterspy (1953) was based.

It has been said that the Avengers character Cathy Gale was created by Doreen Montgomery, screenwriter of this film. As well as writing for the Avengers Montgomery wrote for Danger Man and many other TV series.

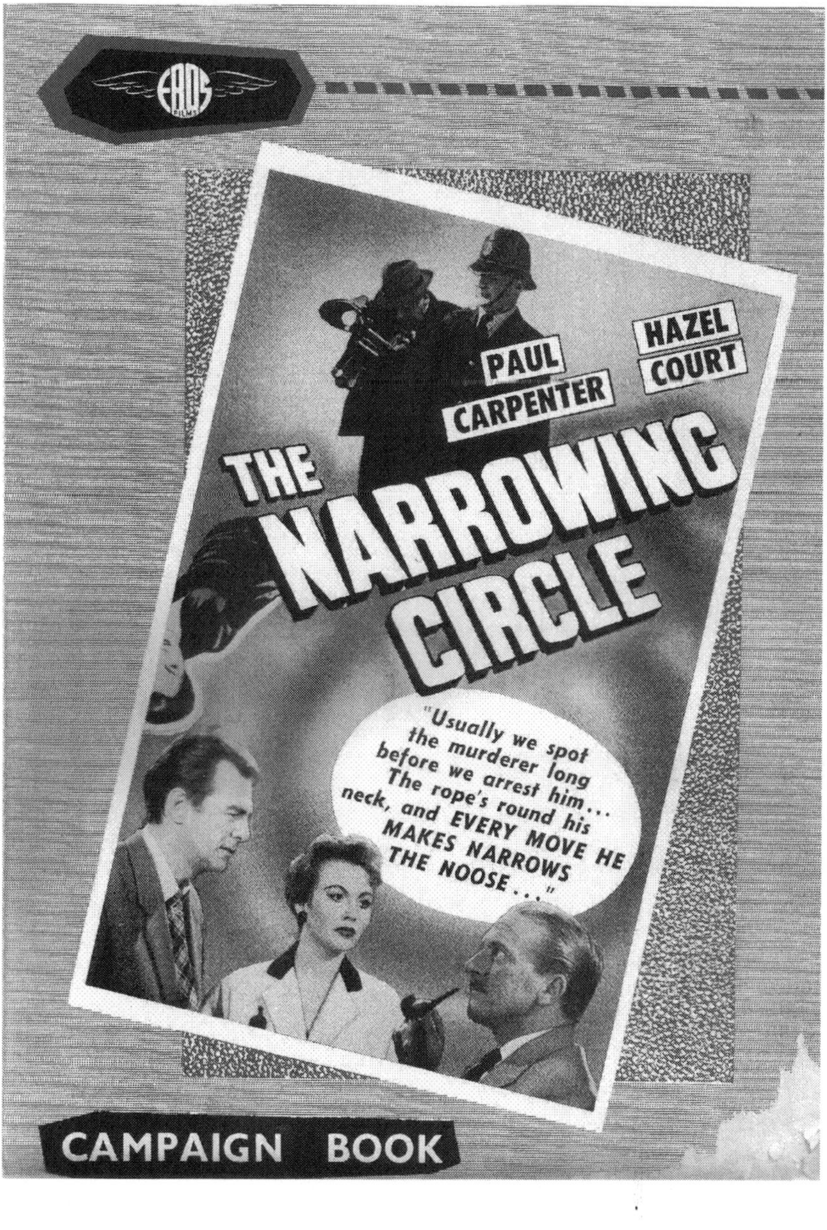
PAUL CARPENTER
HAZEL COURT
THE NARROWING CIRCLE
"Usually we spot the murderer long before we arrest him... The rope's round his neck, and EVERY MOVE HE MAKES NARROWS THE NOOSE..."
CAMPAIGN BOOK

THE INTIMATE STRANGER (aka Finger of Guilt – 1956)

Directed by Joseph Losey – as Joseph Walton (The Servant, The Go-between)

Screenplay by Howard Koch – as Peter Howard (originally titled Pay the Piper)

Produced by Alec C Snowden

Starring: Richard Basehart, Mary Murphy, Constance Cummings, Roger Livesey

Reggie Wilson (Basehart) was a film editor in the USA until an affair with his boss's wife forced him to move away. He gets a job at a British film studio as a producer and is married to Lesley (Faith Brook) who is the boss's daughter. He then starts to get letters from a woman called Evelyn (Murphy) in Newcastle who claims to have had an affair with him in the USA and wants to see him. He and his wife go to Newcastle to confront her, but she is so convincing about her story even he begins to wonder if it did actually happen and doubts his own memory and sanity.

Another ex-girlfriend of Reggie's is an actress named Kay Wallace (Cummings) whom he'd had an affair with in the States and who still has feelings for him. She is working on a film at the studio and in desperation he even confides in her. As his career and marriage hang in the balance Reggie struggles to keep a hold on what is true and what is not – or is he self-delusional? Some imaginative camerawork and effects, particularly in the last few scenes and a nice twist at the end.

Locations: no Merton Park locations, and even the exterior scenes of the fictional film studios were not shot there, but at Shepperton – probably because they needed studios that looked bigger.

Notes: Interestingly, both the director and the screenwriter used pseudonyms because they had been blacklisted in Hollywood during the McCarthy era. Losey had been a member of the Communist party and he, Koch and other American film people came to live in London. Losey used his first two names, Joseph Walton and Howard Koch used the name Peter Howard.

Losey went on to direct The Servant (1963), and The Accident (1967), both starring Dirk Bogarde, and The Go-Between (1971) starring Julie Christie and Alan Bates. He also directed another film at Merton Park, The Criminal (1960) starring Stanley Baker.

Howard Koch had been one of the screenwriters for Casablanca (1942) starring Humphrey Bogart and Ingrid Bergmann and The Sea Hawk (1940) starring Errol Flynn.

Just three years earlier, Mary Murphy had starred with Marlon Brando in The Wild One (1953). She also made another film at Merton Park, The Electronic Monster (1957).

The production designer for this film was artist Richard Macdonald who was uncredited as he was not in the appropriate union. He went on to work on films such as The Servant (1963) and Far From the Madding Crowd (1967) as well as Losey's other Merton Park film, The Criminal (1960).

The posters for the film show Alec C Snowden as producer and director. The actual director, Joseph Losey, is not mentioned. However, a feature in Kinematograph Weekly (1/12/55) says the film was directed by Joseph Walton, Losey's pseudonym. The article also gives the name of the film as With All My Heart which must have been an early working title.

THE CASE OF THE MUKKINESE BATTLE-HORN (1956)

Directed by Joseph Sterling (Operation Conspiracy, Errol Flynn Theatre TV series)

Screenplay by Harry Booth, Jon Penington, Larry Stephens (from an original story by Larry Stephens), plus additional material by Peter Sellers and Spike Milligan

Produced by Michael Deeley (Italian Job, Blade Runner, Deer Hunter)

Starring: Peter Sellers, Spike Milligan, Dick Emery

Some cite this as the best film ever made at Merton Park. A black and white comedy short (just under 30 minutes), it is really a spoof of the Scotland Yard series made here from 1953 to 1961.

Superintendent Quilt (Sellers) and Sergeant Brown (Milligan) are called to a museum by the curator (Emery) to investigate the theft of the rare and valuable Mukkinese Battle-Horn.

The hapless and incompetent pair then set off to find the culprit, making enquiries at various places including a pawnbroker's shop (run by Goon show characters Henry Crun and Minnie Bannister) and a nightclub.

The film is full of sight gags, puns and typical Goonish humour, including Milligan going into Eccles mode, even though it is not billed as a Goons film. Sellers, Milligan and Emery each play several characters and are obviously having a lot of fun in the process.

It is interesting to see that Sellers' police inspector looks very much like the Inspector Clouseau character that he played many years later, with a similar hat, moustache and belted white raincoat, though producer Michael Deeley says this was really a generic police inspector look.

Michael Deeley also said that Harry Secombe did not appear in the film as the budget wouldn't extend to his fee as well as Sellers' and also at this point Secombe's singing career was becoming successful.

Locations: the exterior of Wimbledon art college (in nearby Merton Hall Road) is used.

Notes: This was Michael Deeley's first film and he went on to have an illustrious career, producing big budget films such as The Italian Job, Blade Runner and The Deer Hunter, though he says Mukkinese Battle-Horn was the most profitable film he made, bringing in revenue twenty times the cost of making the film.

Screenwriter Larry Stephens had been a regular co-writer with Spike Milligan on the Goon show and died at the tragically young age of 35.

The Goon Show website mentions the three Goons films that preceded this, Penny Points to Paradise, Let's Go Crazy and Down Among the Z Men, but rates this the best of the lot.

When Monty Python's Holy Grail film was screened at cinemas in 1975 Mukkinese Battle-Horn was the supporting feature.

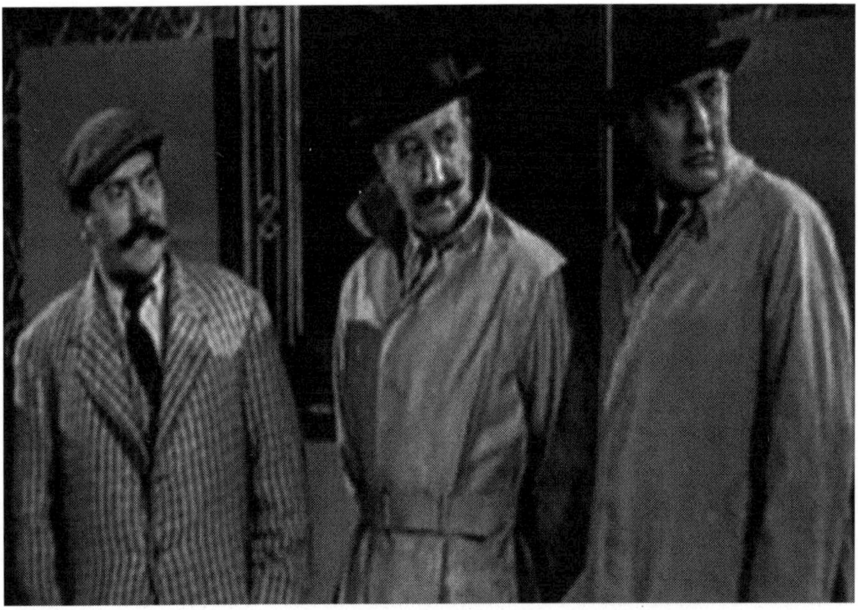

THE HYPNOTIST (aka Scotland Yard Dragnet – 1957)

Directed by Montgomery Tully (Query, Third Alibi, Who Killed the Cat)

Screenplay by Montgomery Tully (based on a play by Falkland L Cary)

Produced by Alec C Snowden

Starring: Roland Culver, Patricia Roc, Paul Carpenter

Test pilot Valentine Neal (Carpenter) has a plane crash and suffers memory loss. He goes to a psychiatrist (Culver) who uses hypnotism to cure him and insists that he stays at his flat during the treatment. At one point though, he wanders off around London, meets a girl in a nightclub and has only the haziest idea of who he is. Eventually he finds his way back but there is a murder in the flat above and he becomes implicated.

A good, atmospheric little thriller which keeps the viewer guessing until the last.

Locations. No outside shooting in Merton Park area.

Notes: The nightclub scene features Chris Barber's jazz band playing a couple of numbers, and is especially interesting as in the background you can see his banjo player, Lonnie Donegan, who was soon to leave the band and concentrate on his highly successful and influential solo career as a skiffle star, which was well underway by the time this film was released in July 1957.

In the US the title of the film was Scotland Yard Dragnet, which is interesting as Montgomery Tully, director of this film also directed many of the episodes of the Scotland Yard series made at Merton Park.

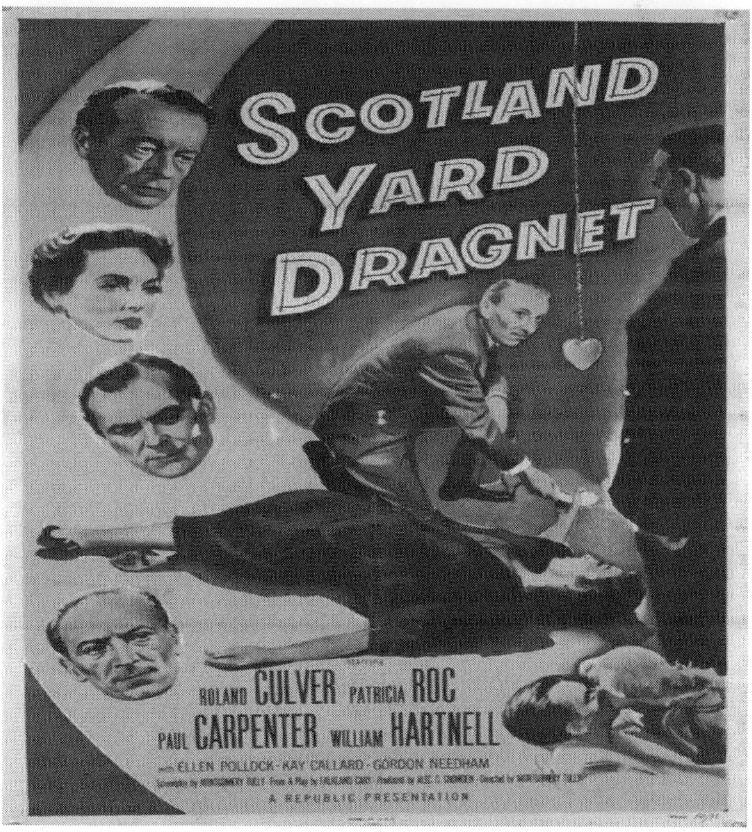

COUNTERFEIT PLAN (1957)

Directed by Montgomery Tully (Boys in Brown, Battle Beneath the Earth)

Screenplay by James Eastwood

Produced by Alec C Snowden

Starring: Zachary Scott, Peggie Castle, Mervyn Johns

Criminal and murderer Max Brant (Scott) escapes the gallows when sprung by members of his gang from a prison van in France. He looks up an old associate, Louie Bernard (Johns), who is a retired master forger and whom he coerces back into working for him in a counterfeiting enterprise. When Louie's daughter visits, she finds out what is going on and is prevented from leaving.

When the police get onto them the gang aren't going to give up without a fight and the film ends on a violent note. In fact, for its time it is quite a violent film, with Scott relishing the brutal and controlling character that he plays.

The film also includes a couple of other Merton Park stalwarts, the Canadian Lee Patterson, playing a gang member, and Sydney Tafler as a rather posh criminal. A good, taut thriller with Scott providing a palpably menacing lead role.

Locations: no Merton Park locations.

Notes: The film poster blurb reads: 'The sensational bullet-blasting inside story of the world's biggest counterfeit ring.'

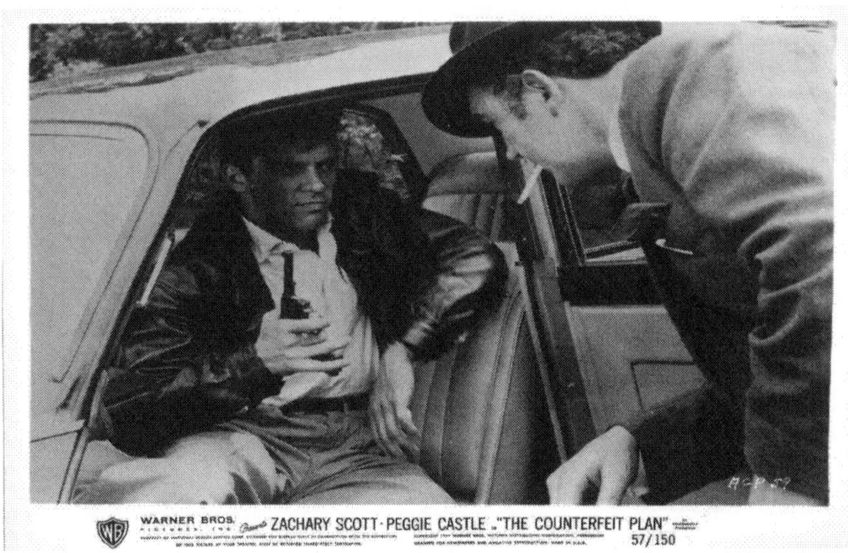

MAN IN THE SHADOW (aka Violent Stranger – 1957)

Directed by Montgomery Tully (Boys in Brown, Battles Beneath the Earth, House in Marsh Road)

Screenplay by Stratford Davis

Produced by Alec C Snowden

Starring: Zachary Scott, Faith Domergue, Gordon Jackson, Kay Callard

Capri barber Carlo Raffone (Peter Illing) goes to the bedside of a man named John Sullivan (Scott) who is apparently dying, and who makes a confession to a murder. Raffone goes to Sullivan's hotel room and finds newspaper cuttings relating to a murder in England and a statuette stained with blood. He flies to England hoping to be able to exploit the situation to his own advantage. He meets a woman whose husband is facing execution for the murder and demands money to reveal the identity of the real killer.

Meanwhile, Sullivan makes a miraculous recovery, finds that the statuette has been stolen and follows Raffone to England ...

Locations: no Merton Park locations; some filming done in Capri according to publicity handouts at the time.

Notes: the film was retitled Violent Stranger in the US as there was another film entitled Man in the Shadow being released that year starring Orson Welles.

The publicity material for the film suggested cinemas arranged tie-ins with local travel agents showing pictures of Capri alongside publicity for the film. It also suggested tie-ins with tailors and menswear shops using slogans such as 'Don't be a Man in the Shadow, get your Spring suit here.'

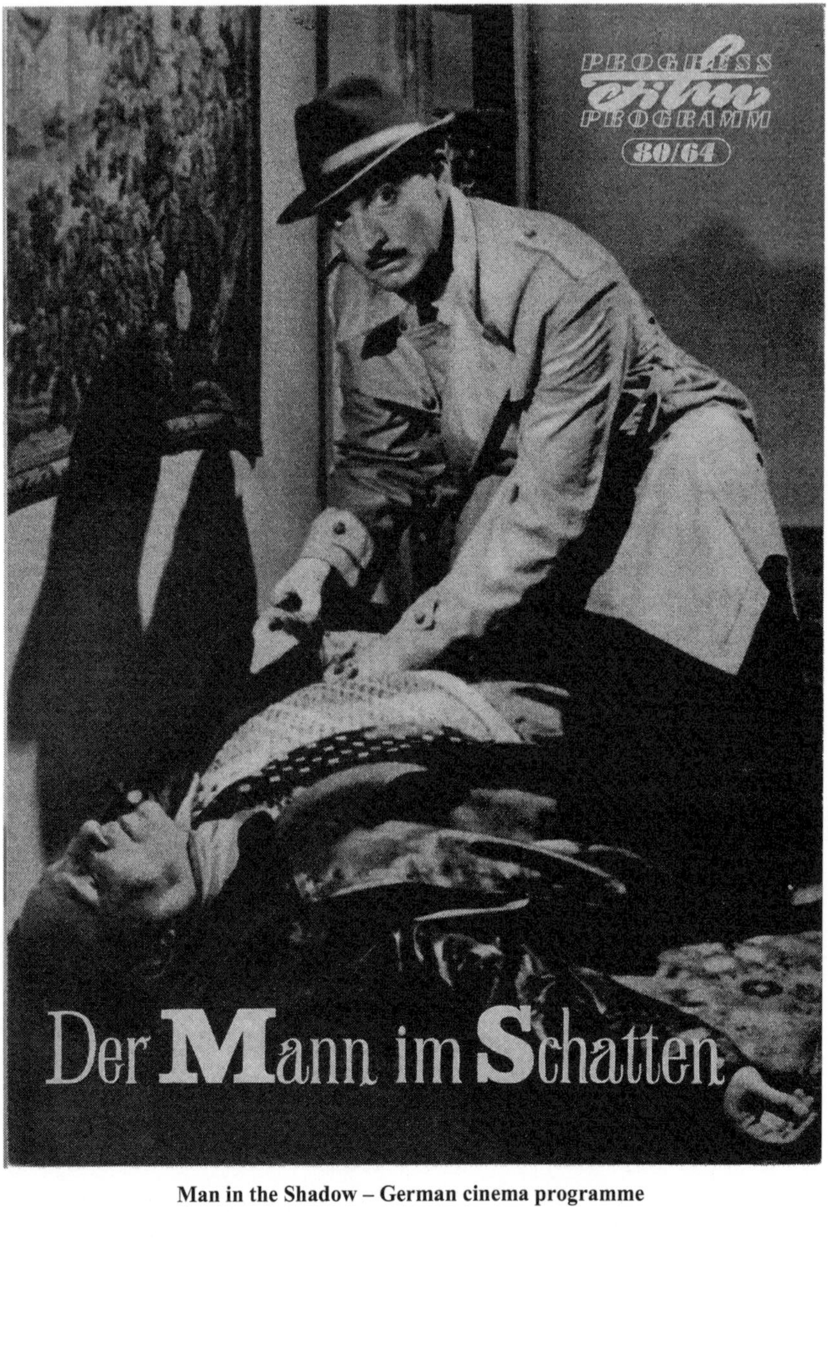

Man in the Shadow – German cinema programme

THE CROOKED SKY (1957)

Directed by Henry Cass (Last Holiday, The Glass Mountain)

Screenplay by Norman Hudis (based on an original story by Charles F Vetter [as Lance Hargreaves] and Maclean Rogers)

Produced by Richard Gordon (uncredited) and Bill Luckwell

Starring: Wayne Morris, Karin Booth, Anton Diffring, Bruce Seton

A gang of counterfeiters are flooding the market with fake five pound notes and the police believe that an American airline is being used to transport the counterfeit cash.

This gives the film makers an excuse to put an American (Morris) in the lead role as Mike Conlin, an investigator posing as an efficiency expert.

Anton Diffring is on characteristically evil form as one of the gang leaders and Bruce Seton plays a Scotland Yard detective who helps Conlin in his investigations.

Not a bad film, with some decent action scenes, a dash of wit, and a variety of settings but with this cast it could have been better had it had more pace.

Locations: no external Merton Park locations seem to have been used.

Notes: The publicity material for the film included the following blurb:

'BREATHTAKING! The Heights of Suspense-Action!'

'A great international forgery blazes across a no man's land of pitiless blue sky!'

Bruce Seton often played police officers and was perhaps best known as 'Fabian of the Yard'.

Writer Norman Hudis later wrote several scripts for the Carry On films, including the first in the series, Carry On Sergeant, the year after this film was made).

Uncredited co-producer Richard Gordon produced several other Merton Park films including Devil Doll (1964) and Horror Hospital (1973).

THE KEY MAN (aka Life At Stake – 1957)

Directed by Montgomery Tully (Boys in Brown, Battles Beneath the Earth, House in Marsh Road)

Screenplay by J McClaren Ross

Produced by Alec C Snowden

Starring: Lee Patterson, Hy Hazell, Colin Gordon

An atmospheric thriller with some central London location filming and a strong cast. Lee Patterson plays a crime reporter who is investigating a missing criminal and the whereabouts of the proceeds of a robbery he committed before spending twelve years in prison.

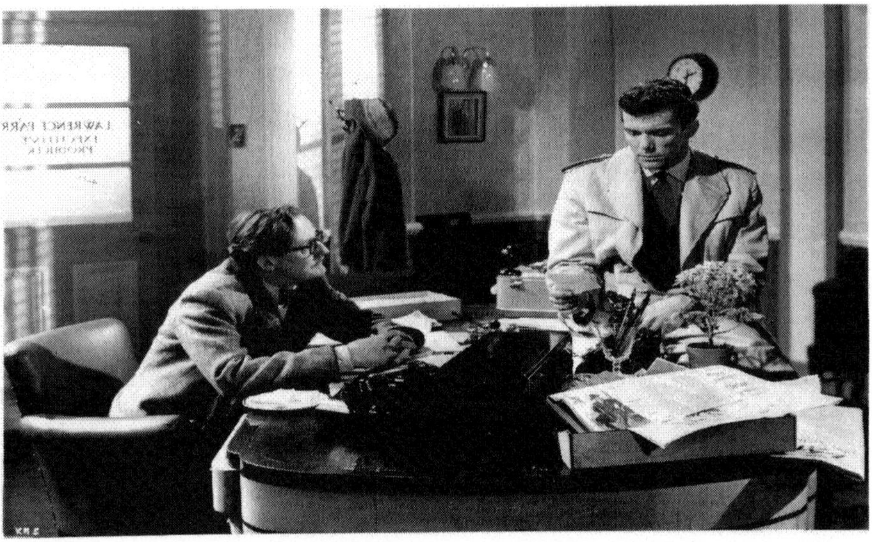

This involves run-ins and fights with various unsavoury London underworld characters while trying to hold his debt-ridden marriage together. Luckily he has an understanding boss (nicely played by Gordon) who is prepared to sub him the funds to complete his investigations.

Some effective scenes, such as the fight in the barber's shop lit only by a pulsating neon sign, and a car chase at the end.

Locations: apart from some filming on the streets of central London, there is also some location work just across the road from Merton Park studios. The car chase at the end shows the Nelson hospital in Kingston Road SW19, the Merton Park Parade of shops and also the Leather Bottle pub which was a favourite with casts and crews over the many years that the studios were here.

Notes: The US title was Life at Stake.

STRANGE AWAKENING (aka Female Fiends, Operation Redhead, Requiem For a Redhead, Wild Women on the Prowl – 1958)

Directed by Montgomery Tully (Boys in Brown, House in Marsh Road)

Screenplay by J McLaren Ross (based on the book Puzzle For Fiends by Patrick Quentin)

Produced by Alec C Snowden

Starring: Lex Barker, Carole Mathews, Lisa Gastoni

Peter Chance (Lex Barker) has amnesia after being attacked by a hitchhiker and is then fooled into thinking that he is heir to a fortune. The three women (the 'female fiends' of the film's alternative title) have their own reasons for leading him to believe this and pose as members of his family as part of the subterfuge.

The film is rather slow and wordy but has its moments of action and humour.

Locations: there are no Merton Park locations used, just studio work.

Notes: Lex Barker played Tarzan in several films before starring in this.

In the UK the film was the supporting feature to 6.5 Special, a musical film based on the TV series of the same name starring Lonnie Donegan and Petula Clark, both of whom had appeared in Merton Park films.

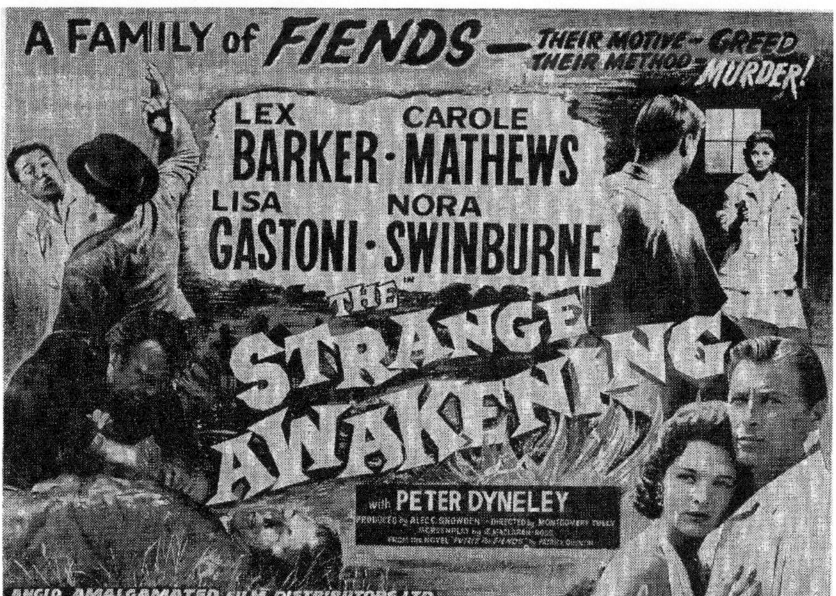

MAN WITH A GUN (1958)

Directed by Montgomery Tully (Battles Beneath the Earth, House in Marsh Road)

Screenplay by Michael Winner

Produced by Jack Greenwood

Starring: Lee Patterson, Rona Anderson, John Le Mesurier, Glen Mason

A good little gangland thriller with a strong cast and notable for being Michael Winner's first full-length screenplay (at the age of 22). It is also notable for including singer Glen Mason, who has something of a cult following.

It is quite short, at just an hour, but has plenty of atmosphere and a decent enough plot.

It starts stylishly with a jazz band and singer (Mason) playing at the nightclub belonging to Harry Drayson (Le Mesurier). One of Drayson's other clubs had burned down just after he took out an insurance policy on it and American insurance investigator Mike Davies (Patterson) comes to look into it. He, and we, soon discover that a criminal gang is involved in trying to muscle in on Drayson's little empire.

The film has plenty of recognisable faces from well-known films, such as Marne Maitland, who appeared in I'm All Right Jack with Peter Sellers the following year, and Bill Nagy, who went on to appear in Goldfinger.

Locations: None in Merton Park area as far as can be established.

Notes: This was the first film for which Ron Goodwin supplied the music. He went on to compose music for films such as Where Eagles Dare, and Hitchcock's Frenzy. Glen Mason wrote both the songs he sings in the film, Fall in Love and I Don't Know and released them both as singles.

THE LONG KNIFE (1958)

Directed by Montgomery Tully (Boys in Brown, Battles Beneath the Earth, House in Marsh Road)

Screenplay by Ian Stuart Black (based on the novel by Leslie Seldon Truss)

Produced by Jack Greenwood

Starring: Joan Rice, Sheldon Lawrence, Dorothy Brewster

Nurse Jill Holden (Rice) has a wealthy patient who is being blackmailed and she gets drawn into the underworld herself.

Locations: another of the few Merton Park films not available on DVD, so locations unknown.

Notes: a couple of years later Sheldon Lawrence appeared in Too Hot to Handle (1960) starring Jayne Mansfield. Ellen Pollock, who appears in this film turned up in Merton Park's last feature film Horror Hospital (1973).

THE ELECTRONIC MONSTER (aka Escapement – 1958)

Directed by David Paltenghi and Montgomery Tully

Screenplay by Charles Eric Maine

Produced by Alec C Snowden

Starring: Rod Cameron, Mary Murphy, Meredith Edwards, Peter Illing

Oscar-winning American film star Clark Denver crashes his car at high speed while in France and insurance investigator Jeff Keenan (Cameron) goes over to find out whether it was an accident or suicide. He finds that the actor had been having controversial electronic brain treatment and wonders whether that could have contributed to his death.

The clinic where he had the treatment is being run by Paul Zakon (Illing) who is using technology developed by scientist Dr Philip Maxwell (Edwards) for his own evil ends. Keenan goes rather beyond his role as insurance investigator to get to the bottom of what is going on at the clinic.

Locations: no Merton Park locations, mainly studio. Notes: Rod Cameron was mainly known for westerns and had appeared in films with Hollywood stars such as Gary Cooper and Fred MacMurray. He later appeared in TV western series Laramie (1959–63). Co-director Paltenghi also directed The Tyburn Case, one of Merton Park's Scotland Yard series.

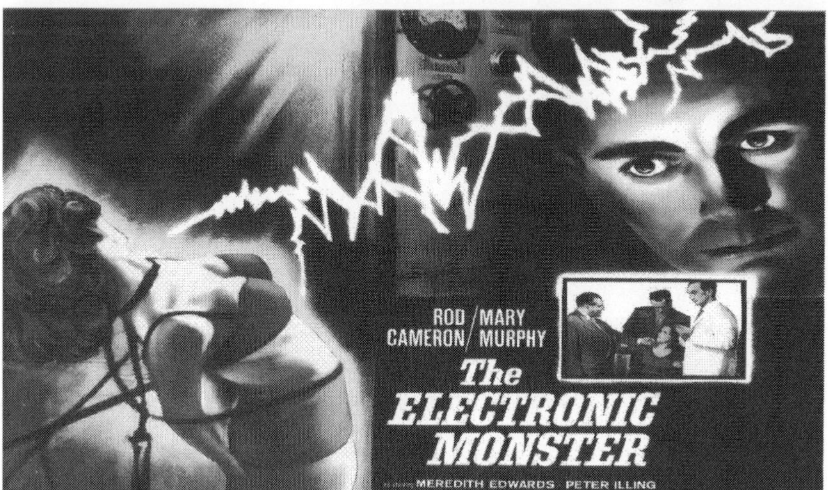

THE WITNESS (1959)

Directed by Geoffrey Muller (The Last Train, Ghost Train Murder, Unseeing Eye)

Screenplay by Julian Bond (based on a story by John Salt)

Produced by Jack Greenwood

Starring: Dermot Walsh, Greta Gynt, Russell Napier, Martin Stephens

A young boy witnesses a crime that his father is accused of. The police use the boy to find the real perpetrators. Another of the few Merton Park films not to have appeared on DVD so full plot details not known.

Locations: not known if any outside filming done in Merton Park.

Notes: Russell Napier plays police inspector Rosewarne. Napier had played a police inspector in many other Merton Park films, mainly in the Scotland Yard series. Screenwriter Julian Bond was the creator of the 1960s Police Surgeon TV series, starring Ian Hendry which was replaced by the more famous Avengers series in which Hendry also played a doctor.

THE WRONG NUMBER (1959)

Directed by Vernon Sewell (The Silver Fleet, Home and Away)

Screenplay by James Eastwood (based on the play by Norman Edwards)

Produced by Jack Greenwood

Starring: Peter Reynolds, Olive Sloane, Lisa Gastoni, Peter Elliot

A gang of criminals led by urbane mastermind Dr Pole (Elliot) robs a mail van and inadvertently kills one of the drivers. Meanwhile, an old lady named Miss Crystal (Sloane) who lives alone with her dog misdials a phone number and speaks to gang member Maria (Gastoni) who gives away vital information that could lead to the gang's whereabouts.

Maria is the girlfriend of Dr Pole but is having an affair with gang member Angelo (Reynolds) who increasingly resents Pole's controlling ways and continuing relationship with Maria.

Olive Sloane is really the star of the film as the dotty old lady, particularly her amusing exchanges with police Superintendent Blake (John Horsley).

All in all a very entertaining film.

Locations: no Merton Park locations.

Notes: that same year Olive Sloane also appeared in Cliff Richard's first film, Serious Charge (1959). She had been a star of the silent films, her first being in 1921.

Also that year, Peter Elliot had appeared in Operation Amsterdam (1959) with Peter Finch and Eva Bartok and also in an uncredited role in Ben Hur (1959). He was known in the 1970s for his role as Doc Morrissey in TV comedy series The Rise and Fall of Reginald Perrin.

The previous year, Lisa Gastoni had appeared in another Merton Park film, Strange Awakening (1958).

THE DESPERATE MAN (1959)

Directed by Peter Maxwell (Ghost Train Murder, Long Shadow)

Screenplay by James Eastwood (based on the novel by Paul Somers)

Produced by Jack Greenwood

Starring: Conrad Phillips, Jill Ireland, William Hartnell, Charles Gray

Crime reporter Curtis (Phillips) is on holiday near an old castle and when he goes to look around he meets Carol Bourne (Ireland), a reporter for a regional newspaper who is investigating the strange story of a cannonball that has gone missing from the grounds.

When they get inside the castle they find a dead body and, not long afterwards, the murderer, jewel thief Smith (Hartnell) who keeps them prisoner in the castle.

Hartnell is good as the criminal and there are moments of tension, but from time to time the drama is allowed to flag and could have done with some tighter editing.

Charles Gray gives an entertaining turn as a rival journalist out to impress Carol.

Locations: no Merton Park locations, much of film shot in a real castle, location unknown.

Notes: the following year Charles Gray appeared in The Entertainer (1960) with Laurence Olivier and later in two James Bond films, once as arch-villain Blofeld.

Four years later William Hartnell became the first Dr Who (1963–66).

Jill Ireland appeared in many TV series in the 1960s and was in Death Wish II (1982) with real-life husband Charles Bronson. She had previously been married to David McCallum.

HORRORS OF THE BLACK MUSEUM (1959)

Directed by Arthur Crabtree (The Strange Case of Dr Manning, Death Over My Shoulder)

Screenplay by Aben Kandel and Herman Cohen

Produced by Herman Cohen

Starring: Michael Gough, June Cunningham, Shirley Anne Field, Graham Curnow

Filmed in colour, and also in 'Hypnovista'*, Horrors of the Black Museum has one or two moments that are quite shocking even today.

Michael Gough is on fine form as the evil crime writer Edmond Bancroft who hypnotises his assistant, Rick (Graham Curnow) into committing murders so that he has something to write about. Despite some clunky dialogue and below-par acting by one or two of the supporting cast the film creates atmosphere and tension with some imaginative sets and grisly props.

It was quite a big hit at the time, doing well in the US, where the release date was before that of the UK and across Europe. One critic described the film as one of a 'Sadeian Trilogy' by production company Anglo Amalgamated; the other two being Circus of Horrors and Peeping Tom, both of which were released the following year.

It has been said that there is a copy of this film in the Museum of Modern Art in New York because of a special request by legendary film director Martin Scorsese. Unfortunately this does not seem to be true (see Myths section).

Locations. No Wimbledon/Merton locations, but the fairground scene was filmed at nearby Battersea funfair.

Notes: A record was released to tie in with the film: (Ooh I'm Scared of the) Horrors of the Black Museum by the Nightmares. The B-side was entitled The Headless Ghost and was released to tie in with the Merton Park film of the same name that was the support feature.

According to producer Herman Cohen he originally wanted Vincent Price to play Edmond Bancroft, and also considered Orson Welles.

* Before each screening of the film (in the USA only) there was a thirteen-minute trailer explaining 'Hypnovista'. In it, a 'psychologist specialising in hypnotism', earnestly explains that you are about to see the most 'fantastic advance ever made in the history of motion picture entertainment. A psychological technique, whereby you, seated in the auditorium, actually become part of the action you see on the screen.' Whether it worked or not we shall probably never know but it all added to the sense of occasion and perhaps contributed to the film's considerable success.

As usual, the publicity people had a few tricks up their sleeves. One stunt was to offer a girl $10 to watch a midnight screening of the film alone in the cinema. It was also suggested that an ambulance should be waiting outside emblazoned with the words 'We are ready to administer aid to Miss ... who is inside watching Horrors of the Black Museum.' Another idea was to hand out an Emotional Reaction Report; a card with questions on it such as: Did you sweat (tick either 'lightly' box or 'heavily' box, Are you still trembling? (lightly, or a great deal'). The film was advertised as being in 'blood-curdling color.'

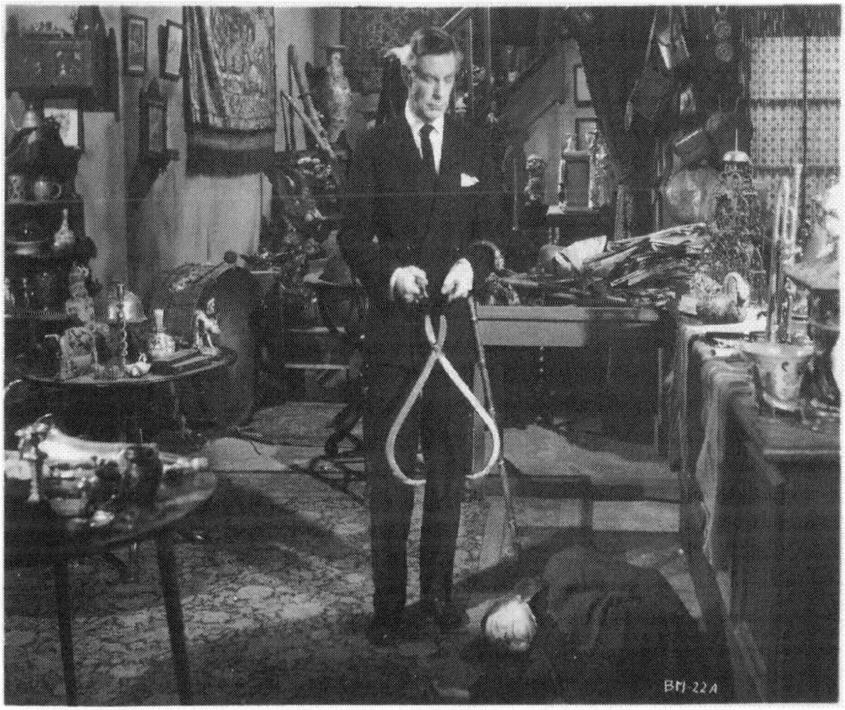

Michael Gough in Horrors of the Black Museum

HIDDEN HOMICIDE (1959)

Directed by Anthony Young (as Tony Young) (Penny Points to Paradise, Hands of Destiny)

Screenplay by Paul Capon (based on his novel Murder at Shinglestrand), Bill Luckwell and Anthony Young

Produced by Bill Luckwell, Derek Winn

Starring: Griffith Jones, Patricia Laffan, Bruce Seton, James Kenney

An intriguing opening as a man named Michael Cornforth (Jones) goes to bed and then wakes up in another house, fully dressed and holding a gun. He then finds the body of his cousin in the house and begins to wonder whether it was he who had shot him. As he struggles to remember, two women walkers call at the house to use his phone, are invited in after some initial reluctance, and one of them finds the body.

One of the women, Jean (Laffan) believes in Cornforth's innocence and begins an affair with him. His cousin's death would result in a substantial amount of money being left to him.

As the plot unfolds we are introduced to several other characters who may or may not be involved in the murder, including a woman who performs in a knife-throwing cowgirl act and the too-nice-to-be-nice Oswald Castellan (James Kenney).

Locations: Plenty of Merton Park area location shooting, including Kingston Road and Merton Hall Road (just yards from the studio), Wimbledon Chase railway station etc. Also, Wimbledon Theatre and possibly some Wimbledon streets too.

Notes: Patricia Laffan had played the eponymous alien in cult classic Devil Girl From Mars (1954).

Bruce Seton was well known by the time of this film for his portrayal of Fabian of the Yard (TV series 1954–56, and film 1954).

Wimbledon Chase station is referred to as 'Wimbledon Station', and someone is even told to meet at the 'Broadway' exit which relates to the latter rather than the former.

One of the other films directed by Tony Young, Penny Points to Paradise, starred Peter Sellers, Harry Secombe and Spike Milligan just before they began the Goon Show on BBC radio.

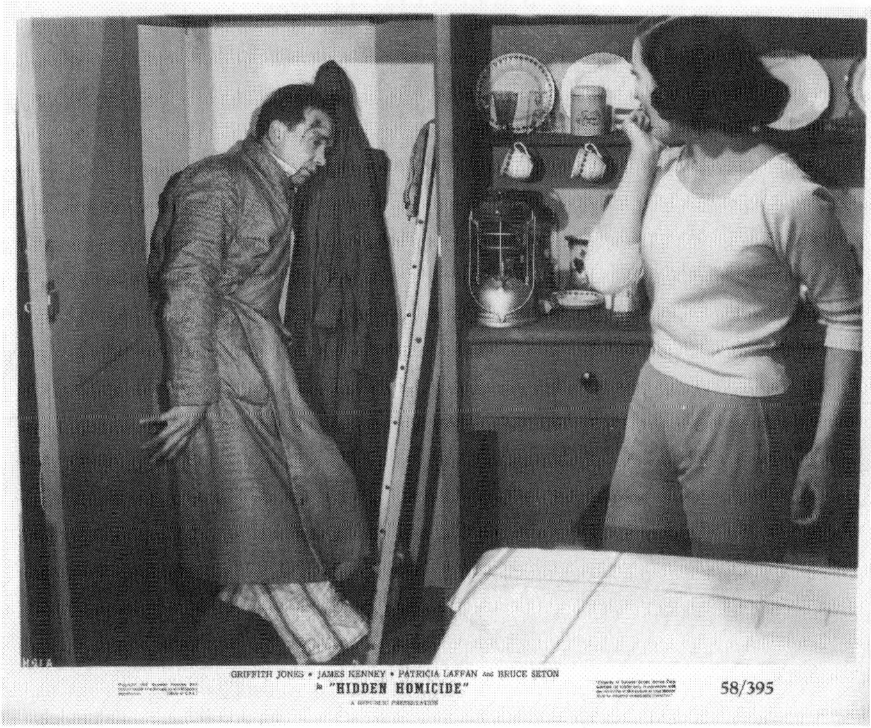

Still from Hidden Homicide (1959)

THE HEADLESS GHOST (1959)

Directed by Peter Graham Scott (Night Creatures, Devil's Bait)

Screenplay by Herman Cohen and Aben Kandel (as Kenneth Langtry)

Produced by Herman Cohen

Starring: Richard Lyon, Liliane Sottane, David Rose, Clive Revill

Not one of Merton Park's better films, and one which even its producer and co-writer Herman Cohen described as a 'bad picture'. It involves three teenagers (two American men and one Danish girl) who have close encounters with various ghosts in an English castle and attempt to reunite the titular ghost's body with its head.

Some of the special effects are quite good, it has some amusing moments and Clive Revill is entertaining as the ghost of the fourth Earl Ambrose, but the film overall is fairly weak and some of the acting rather uninspired.

This is probably because the film was knocked out quickly as a support feature to Herman Cohen's rather better Horrors of the Black Museum (also made at Merton Park in 1959). Cohen had been asked by AIP (American Independent Pictures) to come up with a support feature quickly so that there was a whole package to sell to the US cinema circuits. The screenplay was written in two weeks and the film shot in a further three. Sets from Horrors of the Black Museum were reused and the film was shot in black and white to keep costs down.

A review in the New York Times described it as 'a pale and protracted bit of whimsy'.

Locations: No Merton Park locations used, just studio work. Some filming was done in Allerton Castle, North Yorkshire.

Notes: David Rose, who played one of the teenagers, was also in a CFF (Children's Film Foundation) film, Mystery in the Mine, made at Merton Park that same year (1959). Richard Lyon, the other male teenager, was the son of Bebe Daniels and Ben Lyon and had been in the Life With the Lyons radio show with the rest of the family.

Clive Revill had appeared in Reach For the Sky (1956) with Kenneth More and would later appear in films such as Avanti! (1972) with Jack Lemmon and the Star Wars film The Empire Strikes Back (1980).

Director Peter Graham Scott did a lot of TV work including cult favourites The Avengers and The Prisoner.

The film also spawned a pop record: The Headless Ghost by the Nightmares, a Coasters style comedy record. The other side of the record featured the same group singing '(Ooh I'm scared of the) Horrors of the Black Museum'. Horrors of the Black Museum (1959) was filmed at Merton Park.

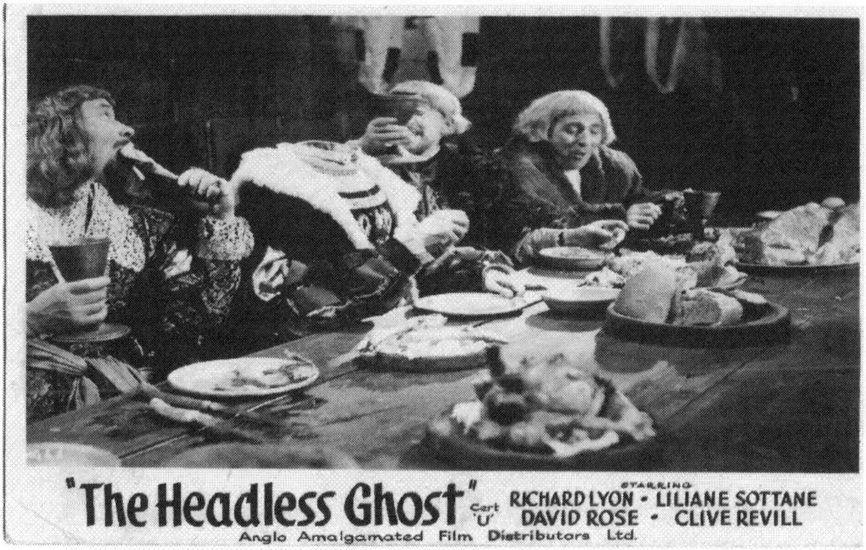

The 'Headless Ghost' doesn't let the lack of a mouth stop him eating

THIRD MAN ON THE MOUNTAIN (1959)

Directed by Ken Annakin (The Longest Day, Those Magnificent Men in Their Flying Machines)

Screenplay by Eleanore Griffin (based on book by James Ramsey Ullman)

Produced by Walt Disney (uncredited) and Bill Anderson

Starring: Michael Rennie, James MacArthur, Janet Munro, Herbert Lom

A Walt Disney production with the rather unlikely filming location combination of Merton Park and the Matterhorn.

Based on a true story, Banner in the Sky by James Ramsey Ullman, it follows a young man's quest to climb the mountain that took the life of his father. A good, wholesome adventure yarn with some stunning scenery and some exciting moments. You have to keep reminding yourself that a good proportion of this film was made in the humble studios of Merton Park.

Anyone who has been on the Matterhorn Bobsleds ride at Disneyland California may be interested to know that it was inspired by this film.

Locations: No Merton Park exteriors in this film!

Notes: Director Ken Annakin's film Those Magnificent Men in their Flying Machines had in its cast several people who had been in Merton Park films: Sam Wannamaker, Gordon Jackson, Terry-Thomas and John Le Mesurier.

THE HOUSE IN MARSH ROAD (1960)

Directed by Montgomery Tully (Boys in Brown, Battles Beneath the Earth)

Screenplay by Maurice J Wilson (based on the play by Laurence Meynell)

Produced by Maurice J Wilson

Starring: Tony Wright, Patricia Dainton, Sandra Dorne, Derek Aylward

Writer David Linton and his wife Jean (Wright and Dainton) are struggling with money partly due to David's drink problem and partly because he can't get settled enough to write. Then out of the blue Jean inherits a house and some money from an aunt who has just died.

They move to the house and quickly find it is haunted by a poltergeist. David hires an attractive woman named Valerie (Dorne) to type his manuscripts and they begin an affair. David then begins to think he must kill his wife if he doesn't want to lose Valerie.

An atmospheric piece with some good acting though the ending is rather anti-climactic.

Locations: this film was not made at Merton Park, but is a Merton Park production. Studio scenes were shot at Walton studios, Walton-on-Thames.

Notes: Montgomery Tully had made many films at Merton Park, including several of the Scotland Yard and Edgar Wallace series.

Sandra Dorne had appeared in Merton Park film Hindle Wakes (1952) and Edgar Wallace film The Malpas Mystery (1960)

Small parts played by Sam Kydd and Olive Sloane.

THE CRIMINAL (aka The Concrete Jungle – 1960)

Directed by Joseph Losey (The Servant, The Go-between)

Screenplay by Alun Owen (based on a script by Jimmy Sangster)

Produced by Jack Greenwood

Starring: Stanley Baker, Sam Wanamaker, Margit Saad, Jill Bennett

From the off this film looks like a classy affair. With busy, long tracking shots and a cool jazz song (Cleo Laine and Johnny Dankworth) being sung over the opening scenes it is clear that we are in the hands of an imaginative director.

The film was quite violent for the time and follows the fortunes (and misfortunes) of Johnny Bannion (Stanley Baker) both inside and outside prison as he plans to reap the rewards of a recent racetrack robbery.

There are some strong supporting roles by Sam Wanamaker, Patrick McGee and Murray Melvin (his screen debut) and the film manages to conjure up the claustrophobic and violent atmosphere of prison life.

Locations: Some filming done in Wandsworth, SW18 including exteriors of Wandsworth prison. One scene is possibly Wimbledon Common.

Notes: Director Joseph Losey had been blacklisted in McCarthy era 50s America and worked both in the UK and continental Europe, sometimes under a pseudonym. In fact, he directed Intimate Stranger at Merton Park in 1956 under the name Joseph Walton (his first two names). Screenwriter Alun Owen went on to write the screenplay for the Beatles' first film, A Hard Day's Night.

The song sung over the opening credits, Thieving Boy by Cleo Laine and Johnny Dankworth (written by Dankworth and Alun Owen) was released on the B side of a single coupled with Let's Slip Away which featured in the film Saturday Night and Sunday Morning. Dankworth also released four instrumental tracks from the Criminal on an EP. The pianist on these instrumental tracks was Dudley Moore, just prior to his involvement with the ground-breaking satirical show Beyond the Fringe.

Sam Wanamaker, as well as having many acting and directorial roles went on to become instrumental in recreating Shakespeare's Globe theatre at Southwark. He had also come to the UK from America fearing blacklisting.

In the USA The Criminal was retitled Concrete Jungle and was billed as 'The Toughest Film Ever Made!'

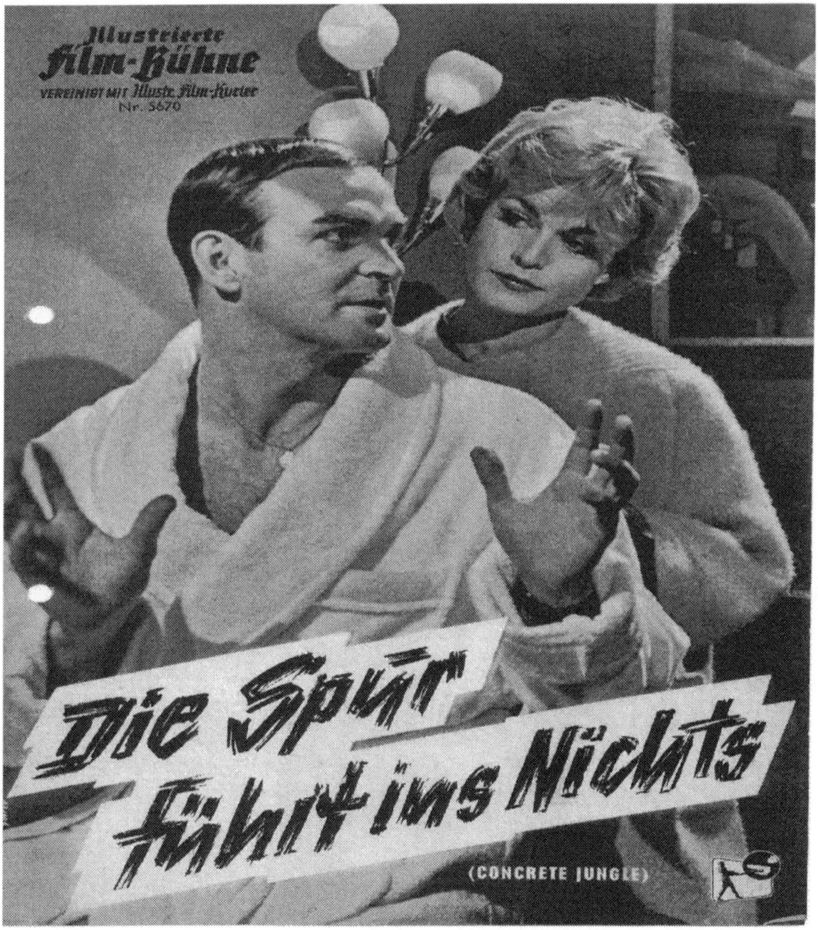

The Criminal (German cinema programme)

KONGA (1961)

Directed by John Lemont (The Shakedown, The Frightened City)

Screenplay by Aben Kandel and Herman Cohen

Produced by Herman Cohen

Starring: Michael Gough, Margo Johns, Jess Conrad, Claire Gordon

Gloriously daft, but great fun if you are willing to suspend your disbelief for ninety minutes.

Clearly inspired by King Kong (1933)* the giant ape in this film runs amok not in downtown Manhattan but on the streets of Croydon – though it is meant to be central London. Also, some of the shops on Merton Park Parade, directly opposite the film studios, were incorporated into the street scenes.

Gough plays botanist Charles Decker who returns from Africa with a pet chimpanzee and a serum from a carnivorous plant that can make living things dramatically increase their size ... what could possibly go wrong? Gough hams it up deliciously and revels in his 'evil' persona.

The film was released in the USA and elsewhere. Confusingly, the Turkish film posters renamed the film King Kong! The working title for the US version was I Was a Teenage Gorilla – a follow-on from two of Konga writer/producer Herman Cohen's previous films, I was a Teenage Werewolf and I was a Teenage Frankenstein (both 1957). Another working title for the film, according to the BFI, was Earth Monster.

But Konga also started something of a mini-industry spawning a novel by Dean Owen (in 1960, before the film was released) and then a series of comic books by American publisher Charlton Comics which ran to 23 issues between 1960 and 1965. There was a 24th issue with a different title: Fantastic Giants, and a spin-off series entitled The Return of Konga which was renamed Konga's Revenge for its third and final issue. There have also been subsequent reprints and collections published right up until 2019. The Konga drawings were by celebrated comic book artist Steve Ditko, who just a couple of years later co-created the Spider-man character for Marvel Comics.

Locations: As mentioned above the shops on Merton Park Parade were used and the shop names remained unaltered for the filming – an early example of product placement?!

Notes: Producer Herman Cohen had to pay RKO $25,000 to use the words 'King Kong' in publicity for the picture. Posters read: 'Not since "King Kong" has the screen exploded with such mighty fury and spectacle!'

* A Merton Park connection here as Edgar Wallace claimed to have been the co-author/creator of King Kong. At the same time as Konga was being filmed the first of 47 Edgar Wallace mysteries was being filmed at Merton Park studios.

Konga was played by actor Paul Stockman who was uncredited on the film. Some sources have stated that Konga was played by George Barrows but although he wasn't, there is a connection. Barrows made something of a career of playing apes, largely due to the fact that he had his own ape costume that he had made himself. He was asked to appear in it in this film but declined, though agreed to lend his ape suit to producer Herman Cohen for someone else to use. Paul Stockman was chosen for two reasons: one, that he was exactly the right height (6 foot) to fit the costume, and two, that he had brown eyes. No one would have believed an ape with blue eyes!

So the gorilla suit was shipped over to Merton Park studios and used in the film, but unfortunately it was damaged and Barrows never lent it out again. Apparently holes had been cut in the suit to aid ventilation and the mechanism that moved the gorilla's lips had been broken.

Interestingly, Barrows did wear the costume himself in the film Black Zoo (1963), the third written and produced by Herman Cohen and starring Michael Gough, following on from Horrors of the Black Museum (1959) and Konga. In some of the publicity material for Black Zoo it is billed as Horrors of the Black Zoo, and some posters show the giant ape, played by George Barrows, making the film look like Konga 2. Cohen said that as soon as the publicity went out with the 'Horrors of the Black Zoo' title interest increased significantly.

As the third of a trilogy of Cohen/Gough films, following Horrors of the Black Museum and Konga, it would have been nice if Black Zoo too had been made at Merton Park studios like its predecessors, but it was in fact made in Hollywood.

No doubt the American studio could better accommodate the large menagerie of wild animals that were central to the film's plot and perhaps it was better for the good citizens of Merton Park to be able to sleep easy in their beds without worrying about any escaped animals (according to the publicity handouts Michael Gough was bitten by a tiger cub, and one of the trainers was so badly bitten by a lion that he needed seventy stitches).

In an interview with the One Show in May 2017 Jess Conrad revealed that he was due to sing a song in Konga but that it was dropped. He confirmed recently that a clip of him singing This Pullover to Claire Gordon was filmed but because the running time of the film was too long something had to be cut, and sadly, it was this song. It was released that year on the B side of his Why Am I Living? Which featured in the film Rag Doll (1961). However, in an interview in Record and Show Mirror on October 1 1960 he said 'I sing in Konga. It's a song called Once Upon a Time and I'll record it so that the release of the disc ties in with the release of the film.' It seems though that this song was not released at all – and it didn't feature in the film.

The American press book for the film reveals that Michael Gough also did book illustrations – including one for poetry book Clear Lake Comes From Enjoyment by Peter Whigham.

Claire Gordon was a friend of Scott Walker and is said to have inspired his song Archangel.

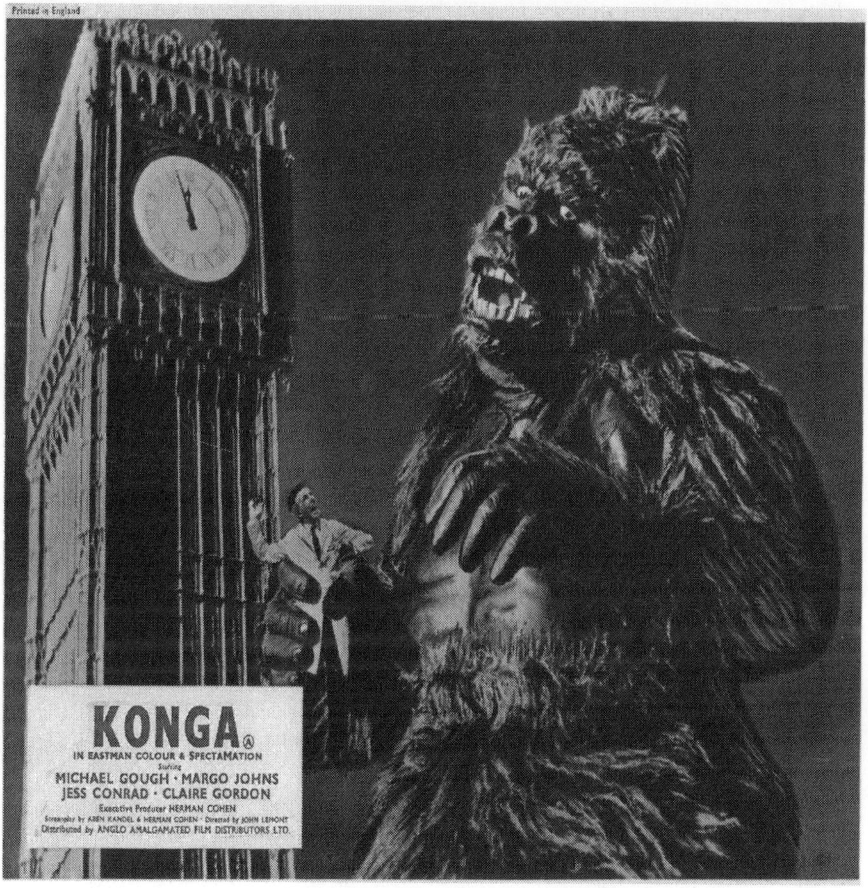

Charles Decker (Michael Gough) is beginning to regret discovering that growth serum

SPARROWS CAN'T SING (1963)

Directed by: Joan Littlewood

Screenplay by Stephen Lewis and Joan Littlewood (based on Lewis's original play, Sparrers Can't Sing)

Produced by Donald Taylor

Starring: Barbara Windsor, James Booth, Roy Kinnear, Avis Bunnage, etc.

Quite a coup for Merton Park studios, this film was directed by Joan Littlewood (the only feature film she ever directed) and starred a dozen well-known actors.

Stephen Lewis's original play, Sparrers Can't Sing was first performed in 1960 at the Theatre Royal, Stratford East by Joan Littlewood's Theatre Workshop.

The location work was filmed in the East End, but the studio scenes were done at Merton Park studios.

The plot is paper-thin (Jack-the-lad Charlie [Booth] comes back from two years at sea to find his wife Maggie [Barbara Windsor] is living with someone else though he is determined to get her back) but is made up for by the sheer vitality and vivacity of the actors who conjure up a post-war East End that is determined to enjoy life to the full despite the poverty and damage from both bombs and town-planners.

At times there is an improvised/documentary feel which has echoes in later work by Ken Loach and Mike Leigh. The natural feel of much of it is also achieved by the use of real East Enders as actors and extras. The pub landlady/singer was played by actress Queenie Watts who fulfilled both those roles in real life.

The cast also includes Brian Murphy, George Sewell, Murray Melvin, Yootha Joyce, Arthur Mullard and many other well-known actors. There is also a cameo by Harry H Corbett.

The Kray twins were also involved and apparently kept the locals in order while filming was going on. Some sources claim that they actually appear in the film towards the end when a fight breaks out in the pub. This scene was actually filmed at Merton Park studios and according to a film expert on the 2017 DVD the Krays did not appear. Interestingly though, the assistant director on this film, Peter Medak, ended up as director of the film The Krays in 1990.

The film even had a royal premiere in Mile End which was attended by Anthony Armstrong Jones (Princess Margaret was unable to attend due to flu) and even did well in the USA. It was the first British film to be screened there with English subtitles to help Americans make sense of the Cockney accents!

The New York Times sniffed 'This isn't a picture for anyone with a logical mind or an ear for language. The gabble of Cockney spoken here is as incomprehensible as the reasoning of those who speak it.'

Barbara Windsor was nominated for a BAFTA for Best Actress (the winner was Rachel Roberts in This Sporting Life).

The title song was written by Lionel Bart and sung by Barbara Windsor and released as a single. There had, incidentally, been a single released in 1961 entitled Sparrers Can't Sing, an instrumental by the Roland Shaw Orchestra and written by someone named Franklyn. This would have coincided with the original play's transfer to Wyndham's theatre in the West End.

The film also had two promotional tie-ins, one with Mann's beer and one with the Milk Publicity Council – which had suggested that the film could be promoted on milk floats!

Locations: No Merton Park exteriors, all done in East End.

Notes: James Booth later starred in Zulu which included two other actors who had appeared in Merton Park films: Stanley Baker (The Criminal 1960) and Michael Caine (Solo For Sparrow 1962). In 1990 screenwriter Stephen Lewis appeared in The Krays film – after all, they did almost appear in his!

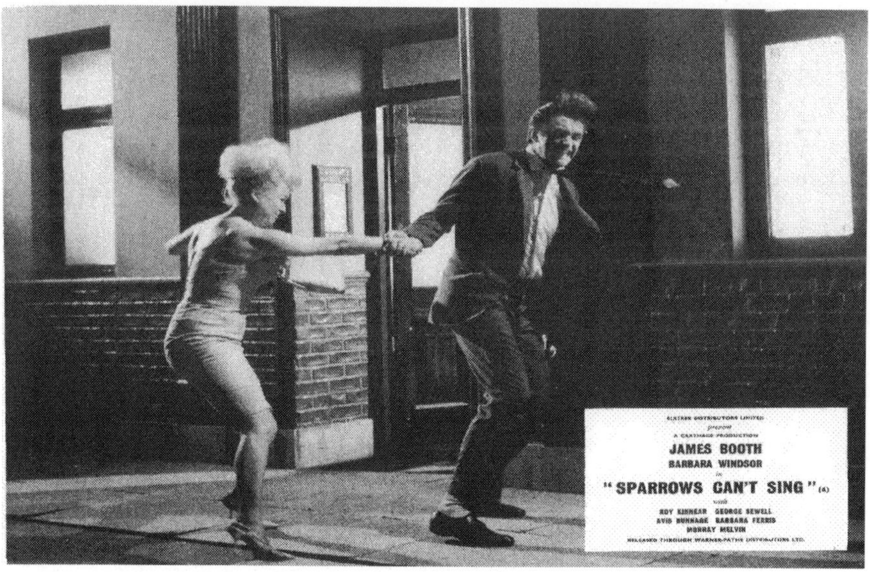

Barbara Windsor and James Booth in a typically tempestuous scene

DEVIL DOLL (1964)

Directed by Lindsay Shonteff (Voodoo Blood Death, The Yes Girls)

Screenplay by Ronald Kinnoch and Charles F Vetter

Produced by Richard Gordon, Kenneth Rive, Lindsay Shonteff, Gerald A Fernback

Starring: William Sylvester, Bryant Haliday, Yvonne Romain, Sandra Dorne

A taut and tense thriller using the now-familiar story of a ventriloquist's dummy (Hugo) that comes to life, but in this film it is not the dummy that is evil but the ventriloquist, the Great Vorelli (Haliday). The ventriloquist is also a hypnotist and uses his powers to take control of the beautiful young Marianne Horn (Romain) who is the girlfriend of American reporter Mark English, who then decides to look into the murky past of the Great Vorelli and his sinister dummy.

Good performances from the strong cast and a neat plot twist at the end help to make this a gripping film which in 1964 would have been quite a scary 'X' certificate cinema experience.

The film also feels rather later than 1964 with Yvonne Romain's later 60s style and some mild nudity that would have been rare in a film of that vintage. In fact, the continental print of the film contained a daring striptease scene that was cut from the UK and US versions.

Locations: As far as can be established there was no location filming done in the Merton Park area, just studio work.

Notes: both William Sylvester and Alan Gifford went on to appear in Stanley Kubrick's 2001, A Space Odyssey (1968) and Yvonne Romain played opposite Elvis Presley in Double Trouble (1967). Bryant Haliday also appeared in another Merton Park film, The Projected Man (1966). Producer Richard Gordon also worked on Merton Park films Horror Hospital (1973) and The Electronic Monster (1958).

The director of Merton Park film The Leather Boys (1964), Sidney J Furie, was offered the role of director on this film but declined, settling instead for The Ipcress File (1965) starring Michael Caine who had appeared in a Merton Park film himself (Edgar Wallace mystery Solo For Sparrow 1962). However, executive producer Richard Gordon said in an interview that Sidney J Furie did indeed work on the film and advised Shonteff throughout but was uncredited.

When the film was released in America the publicists had a range of publicity stunts up their sleeves. They sent out cages containing a Hugo dummy that could be displayed in the foyers of cinemas. There would be a recorded voice giving details about the film. It was also suggested that cinemas could do a tie-in with their local drug stores who would supply smelling salts. There would be a sign in the foyer reading 'Don't faint, take your smelling salts now before you see Devil Doll.' There were also suggestions that girls could be offered a date with Hugo and that vicars could be asked to give quotes regarding the morality of the film.

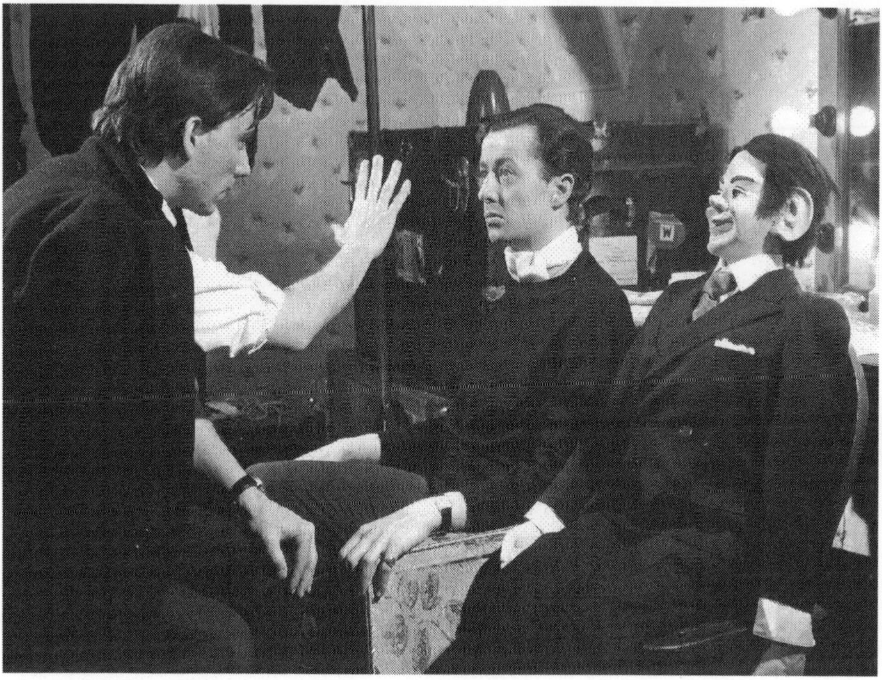

Devil Doll

THE LEATHER BOYS (1964)

Directed by Sidney J Furie (The Ipcress File, Lady Sings the Blues, Superman IV)

Screenplay by Gillian Freeman (based on her book of the same title)

Produced by Raymond Stross

Starring: Colin Campbell, Rita Tushingham, Dudley Sutton

Something of a pioneering film for Merton Park, The Leather Boys tells the story of a gay motorcyclist (Dudley Sutton) and his relationship with newly-married fellow biker Reggie (Colin Campbell).

Based on the 1961 novel of the same name by Eliot George (pen name of Gillian Freeman) the screenplay of this film (also by Freeman) had to tone down the homosexual angle of the plot and concentrate more on the failed teenage marriage between Reggie and Dot (Rita Tushingham) as until the Sexual Offences Act 1967 sexual activity between men was illegal. Even after that it was only legal between men over the age of 21 so the teenage protagonists of this film would still have been acting outside the law anyway.

Some of the dialogue in the film is based on improvisation by the cast encouraged by director Furie though it is said that writer Gillian Freeman was not always in agreement with the scripted dialogue being altered in this way.

The film is also interesting in showing the clash between a liberated young woman (Tushingham) who wants to live a life of fun and freedom and a husband with ingrained old-fashioned attitudes such as expecting his tea to be cooked when he gets home from work.

Despite the rather grim working-class backdrops in a black and white post-war London the film has plenty of moments of humour and fun. When the young couple gets married the entire wedding party goes to the reception by bus with Reggie's uncle buying 43 tickets from the conductress!

The UK release of the film was delayed. Production had been completed by December 1962 and editing by April 1963, but the film was not released until March 1964. At the time there was some controversy about the two big cinema chains, ABC and Rank, ignoring small budget films such as this in favour of bigger ones. It may have been too that there was some disquiet about the subject matter.

The film wasn't released in the USA until November 1965 (by this time director Sidney J Furie's next film, the Ipcress File, had already been released – on August 2) but despite getting some good reviews it was not a big commercial success. It was surprising that the film managed to get a certificate in the USA as the Motion Picture Production Code was still in place and even the toned-down homosexual theme must have given the censors pause for thought. In 1966 the film was nominated for a Golden Globe award in the category of Best English Language Foreign Film, but lost out to John Schlessinger's Darling, starring Julie Christie.

The famous bikers' haunt, The Ace Cafe on the North Circular was used and when the cafe fully reopened in 2001 after closing down in 1969 the ceremony was attended by Rita Tushingham, Colin Campbell, Dudley Sutton and Gillian Freeman.

Locations: The wedding takes place at St Peter's (now Bethel) church, Kohat Road SW19 and the bus taking the guests to the reception goes down Haydon's Road SW19.

Notes: Lead actor Colin Campbell achieved iconic status of a sort when his face was used on the Smiths CD single William it Was Really Nothing, and the German version of their 7″ single Ask in the 1980s. The promotional video of the band's Girlfriend in a Coma (1987) also used footage from the Leather Boys throughout the film. The film also includes a young Johnny Briggs, later more famous as long-standing cast member Mike Baldwin in Coronation Street.

A record was released to tie in with the film, The Eyes of the Young Ones by Danny Street. Although the label states 'from the film The Leather Boys', this sung version was not used in the film, just an instrumental. Director Sidney J Furie had directed the Cliff Richard film: The Young Ones (1961) and was offered the chance to direct Summer Holiday (1963) for him too, but declined in order to avoid early pigeonholing as 'The Cliff Richard director' and instead took on the Leather Boys. Interestingly, Furie did agree to direct Cliff's Wonderful Life (1964) and in doing so missed the chance to direct the first Beatles film A Hard Day's Night which was unfortunate as the films went head to head on cinema release and the Beatles film was the clear winner.

INVASION (1966)

Directed by Alan Bridges (The Hireling, The Shooting Party)

Screenplay by Roger Marshall (based on an original story by Robert Holmes)

Produced by Jack Greenwood

Starring: Edward Judd, Yoko Tani, Valerie Gearon

The only real sci-fi film made at Merton Park studios. Aliens from the planet Lystria land on Earth, and one is an escaped prisoner the others are trying to apprehend. The escapee is run over by a car and taken to a nearby cottage hospital where most of the subsequent action takes place. An invisible force-field barrier is placed around the hospital by the aliens and a very dramatic and effective car crash results from this.

A good thriller with interesting camera work, excellent acting, naturalistic dialogue and plenty of atmosphere, including alien spacecraft in the sky, which belies the low budget.

Locations: There is a fair bit of location filming but it has not been established where this took place. It would have made budgetary sense for some of it to have been done in or near Merton but unfortunately there is no information available.

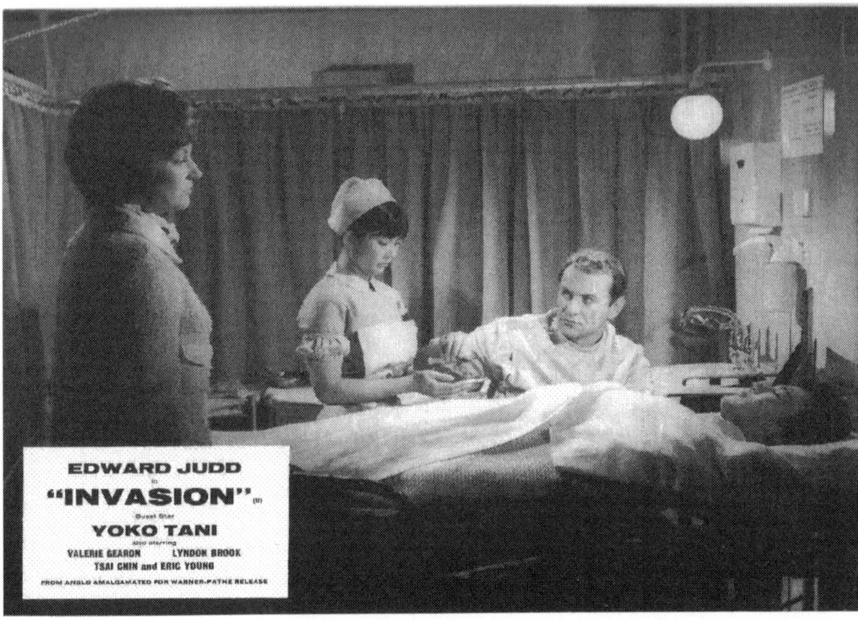

Notes: The writer of the story on which this film is based, Robert Holmes, used the same story as a basis for an episode of Doctor Who in 1970. The episode was entitled Spearhead From Space: Episode 1, and was the first episode in which Jon Pertwee appeared as the Doctor. Holmes also wrote many other episodes of Doctor Who and for many other popular TV series. Yoko Tani made films in the USA, Germany, Italy and France and this is one of the very few she made in the UK, though she also appeared in The Partner (1963), one of the Edgar Wallace films made at Merton Park.

Glyn Houston, who played Police Sergeant Draycott, had also appeared in several other Merton Park films, often as a police officer, including Solo For Sparrow which featured a young Michael Caine.

The film was released in the USA and the pressbook includes plot outlines in French and German. The press book also suggests that to publicise the film a dummy rocket ship could be driven around on a float with two or three people dressed as Lystrians.

THE PROJECTED MAN (1966)

Directed by Ian Curteis, John Croydon (uncredited)

Screenplay by John Croydon (as John C Cooper), Peter Bryan (based on a story by Frank Quattrocchi)

Produced by John Croydon, Maurice Foster

Starring: Bryant Haliday, Mary Peach, Norman Wooland

A scientist develops a way of instantly transporting matter from one place to another and after experiments on inanimate objects he starts on living things, and ultimately on himself. Needless to say, the experiment does not go to plan and he is hideously disfigured. On top of this his previous seething professional grudges and personal jealousies are amplified and he goes on the rampage.

Some good special effects and strong performances from the cast though the film is sadly let down by a weak, and sudden ending.

In the USA the film went out on a double bill with Island of Terror starring Peter Cushing. British actor Sam Kydd was in both films.

The American posters read 'Born a man ... turned into a living laser beam by science's most gruesome experiment!'

In some of the publicity material for the double-bill with island of Terror it said: 'Together ... the horrifying terror twins! Three hours of fantastic fear!'

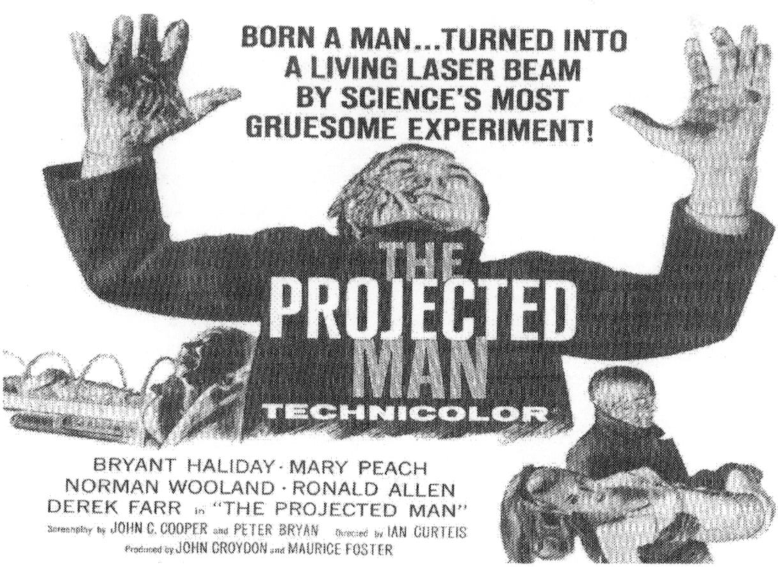

The Projected Man was billed as having 'a billion volts of death in every finger!'

Locations: no location shooting in or around Merton Park, just studio work.

Notes: In the US version the body of a woman is uncovered in a morgue revealing only her face but in the UK and European version the top half of her naked body is shown.

The following year Tracey Crisp, who plays secretary Sheila Anderson, was in the James Bond spoof Casino Royale starring Peter Sellers, David Niven and Ursula Andress.

A couple of years previously Bryant Haliday had starred in another Merton Park horror film Devil Doll (1964).

BINDLE (ONE OF THEM DAYS) (1966)

Directed by Peter Saunders (The Ghoul, Legend of the Werewolf – both as assistant director)

Screenplay by Glyn Jones (Based on the books by Herbert Jenkins)

Produced by Arthur Ferriman

Starring: Alfie Bass, Johnnie Wade, Carmel McSharry, Patrick Newell

According to the Internet Movie Database (IMDb) this was a pilot for a cancelled TV series, but judging by the amount of location shooting and the Eastman colour it may well have been released as a cinema short (it ran at just under an hour). After all, British TV colour transmission wasn't to begin until the follow year, 1967.

The Bindle character began in a series of books by Herbert Jenkins, the first of which was published in 1916. There were several film shorts in the 1920s too but by the 1960s when this was released the humour must have seemed very dated.

Bindle (Bass) is a workshy antiques dealer/market trader who disappears into a pub at every opportunity and forgets about whatever job he is supposed to be doing. He and his mate (Wade) are supposed to be doing a removals job (with a horse-drawn pantechnicon) and manage to lose it and its contents – which includes the client's wife.

Alfie Bass does his best to squeeze some humour out of a rather dreary script and the supporting cast includes some of those character actors whose names you may not remember but whose faces are familiar from many TV appearances from the 1960s onwards. Both Patrick Newell and Johnnie Wade are instantly recognisable from series such as The Avengers and Minder respectively.

Locations: the outside filming does not appear to include any areas local to Merton Park.

Notes: The previous year Bass had a small part in the Beatles' second film, Help! (1965) The madcap and sometimes surreal humour cannot have been much more different to this.

Patrick Newell later appeared in many episodes of TV's The Avengers as the wheelchair using government official named 'Mother'.

Newell had also appeared in one of Merton Park's Edgar Wallace films, Never Mention Murder (1964).

THE FROZEN DEAD (1966)

Directed and produced by Herbert J Leder (It!, Pretty Boy Floyd)

Screenplay by Herbert J Leder

Starring: Dana Andrews, Anna Palk, Philip Gilbert

Mad scientist Dr Norborg (Dana Andrews) freezes the heads of Nazi war criminals so he can graft them onto bodies and let them continue their evil ways. Unfortunately the brains are damaged so he needs a fresh head. One decapitation later he has the head of a woman wired up in his laboratory.

There are times when the film descends into melodrama and the 'evil' German accents become almost comical but there are moments that are genuinely chilling and unsettling, and the special effects work well even though their artifice is sometimes transparent.

The film ends on a bleak and troubling note.

The film is also notable for giving Edward Fox his first credited film role.

Locations: The railway scenes look very much as though they could have been shot at Merton Park station.

Notes: Leading man Dana Andrews had been in films since the 1940s and had starred in Battle of the Bulge with Henry Fonda and Charles Bronson the year before this film.

In the publicity material sent out before the film's release it was suggested that cinemas invest in a large block of ice to put in the foyer with a magician trapped inside! It would of course have to be a magician well-versed in what the publicists called the 'frozen in ice' trick.

They also suggest having the largest fridge that could be found set up in the lobby and inviting members of the public to test their endurance by seeing how long they could bear being in the fridge. No 'health & safety' nonsense in those days!

One other stunt was to put a dummy hand into a tray of ice chunks and walk round the cinema inviting people to 'shake the hand of one of the 'frozen dead'.

In the USA the film was on a double-bill with It!, also written and directed by Herbert J Leder.

IT! (aka The Curse of the Golem, The Anger of the Golem – 1967)

Directed and produced by by Herbert J Leder (Frozen Dead, Pretty Boy Floyd)

Screenplay by Herbert J Leder

Starring: Roddy McDowall, Jill Haworth, Paul Maxwell

The Golem is a mythical Hebrew monster that is brought to life by museum curator Arthur Pimm (McDowall). He tries to control it for his own ends but it seems intent on destruction, with or without his control.

McDowall has a lot of fun with the role, making Pimm by turns innocent, childlike, menacing and neurotic. The character is also given a fixation with his dead mother which instantly recalls Norman Bates in Psycho.

A strong supporting cast makes this a very watchable film though, as always with films of this vintage and this budget, the special effects have their limitations which will require some suspension of disbelief.

Locations: No Merton Park locations (just studio) but uses nearby Hammersmith bridge, Barnes, etc.

Notes: Although Roddy McDowall was still only in his thirties when he made this film, he had been in the business for almost thirty years having appeared in his first film in 1938. He later became best known for his parts in the Planet of the Apes films. Incredibly, the opening credits on this film get his name wrong, billing him as 'Roddy MacDowall.'

The film was also known as The Curse of the Golem and The Anger of the Golem.

Just a few years previously, at the age of fifteen, Jill Howarth had appeared in Otto Preminger's Exodus (1960) alongside Paul Newman and Ralph Richardson and in 1965 in his film In Harm's Way with John Wayne and Kirk Douglas. She also later appeared in Horror House (1969) with two actors who had appeared in other Merton Park films: Dennis Price and Richard O'Sullivan.

A US publicity handout at the time said 'we daren't describe it (the film) to you as you might be afraid to come to the theatre.' It was shown in the US on a double bill with another Merton Park film, The Frozen Dead.

THE CORPSE (aka Crucible Of Horror, The Velvet House – 1971)

Directed by Viktors Ritelis

Screenplay by Olaf Pooley

Produced by Gabrielle Beaumont

Starring: Michael Gough, Simon Gough, Yvonne Mitchell, Sharon Gurney

An atmospheric and effective thriller until about halfway through when the film seems to lose its way somewhat. It does however have a surprise ending which is worth sticking around for.

Michael Gough plays an unpleasant and controlling father that his family of wife, son and particularly his daughter, whom he beats, are wary of. The wife and daughter hatch a plan to get rid of him for good, but will they succeed?

The film has a very effective feeling of claustrophobia which is somehow even achieved on location shooting. The music, by John Hotchkis, also contributes to the queasy and slightly unreal atmosphere.

This appears to be the only film ever directed by Viktors Ritelis who was better known for TV work on series such as The Lotus Eaters and A Country Practice. He also worked on some Doctor Who episodes as did writer Olaf Pooley.

The characterisation by Michael Gough is more restrained than some of his earlier Merton Park horror films which tended towards the more melodramatic demands of 1960s films of that genre.

His son in the film is played by his real-life son and his daughter is played by his son's wife.

Writer Olaf Pooley also appears in the film as Reid.

In the USA the film went out under the title Crucible of Horror, while in Canada it was known as The Velvet House. In the UK it went out under the title The Corpse and was on a double bill with another X film, The Psycho Lover. (When the latter film came out on video in the USA it had three widely disparate alternative titles: The Lovely Touch, The Loving Touch and Psycho Killer. Interestingly the original 1971 British press book for this double bill uses the Psycho Killer title).

Locations: Near the beginning of the film Sharon Gurney is seen cycling into John Innes Park in Mostyn Road SW19, although according to the original press release the family house is supposed to be set in Richmond, Surrey.

Notes: both Michael Gough and Sharon Gurney appeared in Ken Russell's Women in Love which was partly filmed at Merton Park studios (see section entitled Films Made at Merton Park after 1967). Producer Gabrielle Beaumont directed many episodes of well-known US TV series such as Hill Street Blues, Star Trek and Dynasty.

HORROR HOSPITAL (aka Computer Killers – 1973)

Directed by Antony Balch (Bizarre)

Screenplay by Antony Balch, Alan Watson

Produced by Richard Gordon

Starring: Michael Gough, Robin Askwith, Vanessa Shaw

Probably the last film made at Merton Park, it starts with a couple of gory decapitations leavened slightly by some black humour.

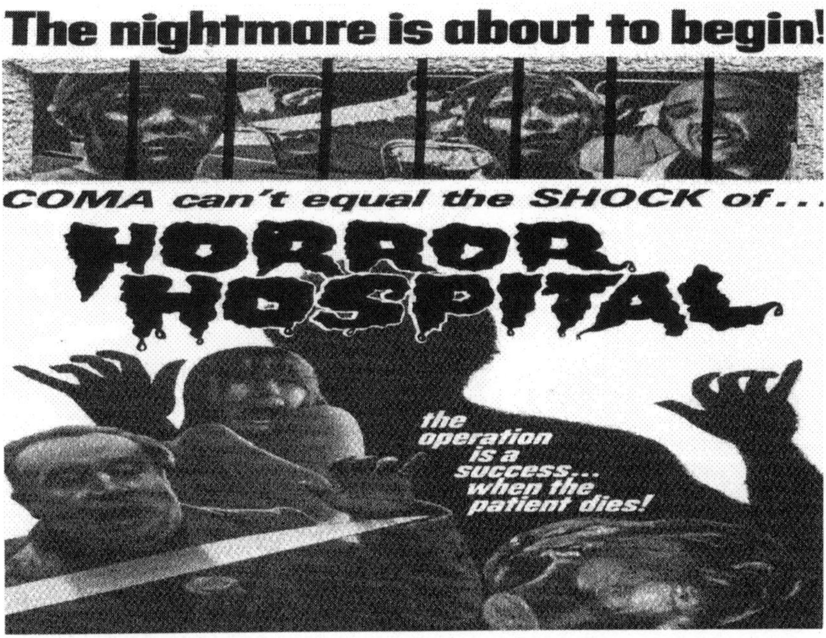

Michael Gough plays the evil Dr Christian Storm who captures and lobotomizes young people for his own ends.

Jason Jones (Askwith) travels down to the evil doctor's lair for a holiday, after picking up a leaflet advertising Hairy Holidays and going to a seedy travel agent's run by an even seedier old lecher (played by Dennis Price). On the train down there Jason meets innocent young woman Judy Peters (Shaw) who is off to the same place to see her Aunt Harris (Ellen Pollock), wife of the evil doctor.

The doctor surrounds himself with a bizarre cast of characters including a dwarf manservant (Skip Martin) and a phalanx of motorcycle-helmeted biker thugs as well as the redoubtable and rather sinister Aunt Harris.

Naturally it all culminates in a battle of good against evil – and there can only be one winner in that can't there?

Michael Gough, as always, is very good playing someone evil and demented and is very watchable but some of the supporting cast's acting is rather one-dimensional though the plot is no dafter than many other horror films of this era.

As it is the 1970s there is some gratuitous nudity and a couple of four-letter words but otherwise there are horror film clichés that could have come from a film two or three decades earlier: a remote house, thunder and lightning, a lugubrious stationmaster at a deserted station, creaking doors, etc.

It is all given a modern twist with the long-haired hero and a pop group scene, not to mention lashings of gore and is seen in some quarters as one the best examples of a British horror film. The britishhorrorfilms.co.uk website calls it 'one of the greatest, if not the greatest, horror films ever made on these islands.'

That is probably something for horror film aficionados to argue about but for the general viewer it might be more of a curiosity; a film very much of its time but with some startling special effects, eccentric characters and dark humour.

In the USA it was apparently titled Computer Killers according to the IMDb but no posters or videos with this title have been found. In fact, producer Richard Gordon says the Computer Killers title was only used for a short while then it reverted to Horror Hospital.

On its cinema release the film was on a double bill with Corpse Grinders.

The film was released on VHS in the USA in 1988 and this time the title was Doctor Bloodbath and the video sported a lurid cover showing a naked woman screaming and the bloody, decapitated heads of two other women.

Locations: Merton Park railway station is used as the fictitious Brittlehurst station and Wimbledon Common is used.

Notes: The pop group at the start of the film was known as The Mystic and performed a song entitled Mark of Death. According to postings on YouTube by the band members themselves they had actually been members of the 60s psychedelic group Tangerine Peel and the song was written by bass player Warwick Rose under the pseudonym Jason de Havilland. The song does not appear to have been released on record.

When released in Germany the film's title was Dr Frankenstein's Horror Klinik and Michael Gough's character was called Dr Frankenstein.

Director and co-screenwriter Antony Balch was a controversial, experimental director who had worked with novelist William Burroughs.

According to the IMDb the part of Abraham (played by Kurt Christian) was originally offered to Nicky Henson.

In a DVD interview producer Richard Gordon says the budget for the film was just £50,000 and various Merton Park studio staff (including the tea lady!) were used as extras.

The US pressbook for the film includes the slogans: 'The nightmare is about to begin!' and 'The operation is a success when the patient dies!' as well as the rather baffling 'Coma can't equal the shock of ... Horror Hospital.'

MISCELLANEOUS

EMERGENCY CALL (aka The Hundred Hour Hunt – 1952)

Directed by Lewis Gilbert (Alfie, Moonraker, Educating Rita)

Screenplay by Vernon Harris and Lewis Gilbert

Produced by Ernest G Roy

Starring: Jack Warner, Anthony Steel Sid James, Freddie Mills

Although this film was made at Nettlefold studios, Walton-on-Thames, the Merton Park dubbing crew was used.

The plot involves a sick child in hospital needing an emergency blood transfusion.

FILMS BY THE THEMERSONS

Polish artists Franciszka and Stefan Themerson were makers of experimental and propaganda films in the 1930s and 1940s, two of which are believed to have been made at Merton Park studios after they managed to escape Nazi-occupied France: The Eye and the Ear (1944/45), and Calling Mr Smith (1943). The latter was a short anti-Nazi film.

In the 1960s Franciszka taught at Wimbledon school of Art, just a short distance from Merton Park film studios.

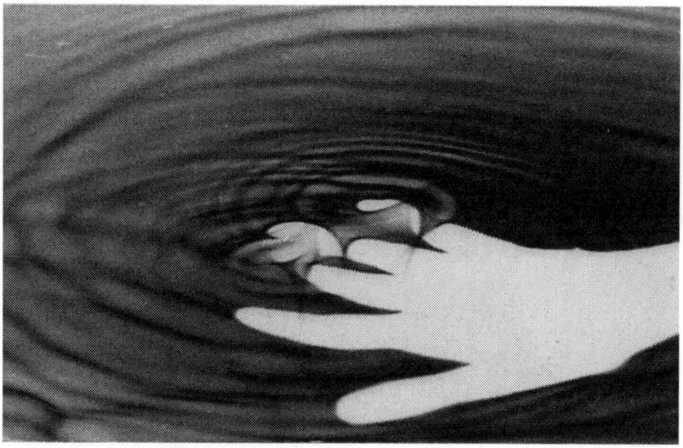

Above: Franciszka and Stefan Themerson, The Eye & The Ear, 10 minute film, London, 1944–45, about the visualisation of sound. Music: four songs by Karol Szymanowski to poems by Julian Tuwim, of which this is an image from poem no.4, 'Wanda'. Copyright, Themerson Estate.

DOCUMENTARIES

Publicity Films, the company that made many advertisement films and documentaries at Merton Park had been in existence for many years before coming here. It had been formed in 1919 by advertising agency The London Press Exchange.

After Sound Services had opened film studios at Merton Park in 1931, Publicity Films moved into part of Long Lodge in 1934. The company named Merton Park Studios Ltd was not formed until 1937.

Over the years, some distinguished producers and directors worked on these early films and included feminist filmmaker Jill Craigie and celebrated director Lindsay Anderson. The films also included well-known actors such as Stanley Holloway and Terry-Thomas.

The earliest one that can be found is The Nightwatchman's story – A Romance of Industry (1933) which was produced for chocolate company Cadbury.

The second was Mastership (1934) – a religious film instigated by J Arthur Rank.

There followed films for Spillers, Shell Mex, Hoover and many other high-street brands.

In 1937 a commercial for Ford Motors was made here which included actor Peter Haddon who went on to become actor-manager of Wimbledon Theatre from 1955 until his death in 1962. The commercial was entitled The Man Who Made Up His Mind.

In 1938 Stanley Holloway starred in a commercial for the Co-Op entitled The Co-Operette and the following year he was in another Co-Op ad entitled Sam Goes Shopping which co-starred Terry-Thomas.

In 1939 a travelogue film, Springtime in the Holy Land was made here. It is just fifteen minutes long and in colour and is now in the Steven Spielberg Jewish Film Archive.

Stanley Holloway starred in a third commercial here in 1940, this time the client was National Savings.

Some of the titles are interesting. In 1940 Persil filmed Every Man His Own Housewife and Potty Politics. In 1941 Kill That Rat! was filmed here, presumably a government information film.

During the war several propaganda films were made for the government with titles such as Give Us More Ships (1941), Salute To Farmers (1941) and More Eggs From Your Hens (1942).

In 1944 Jill Craigie wrote and directed Out of Chaos, a short (28 minutes) film about modern art, featuring the work of Stanley Spencer, Graham Sutherland and Henry Moore. The film also included art historian Kenneth Clark and politician Herbert Morrison.

Director Lindsay Anderson made his first film here in 1948 (Meet The Pioneers) a documentary for the Richard Sutcliffe Limited underground-conveyor company. He was to return many years later to film scenes for If (1968).

The documentaries continued through the 1950s and into the early 1960s and included government information films and educational films. There were also more commercials for companies such as Guinness and Horlicks, but by 1962 the main output was feature films, including the Edgar Wallace mysteries and Scales of Justice series.

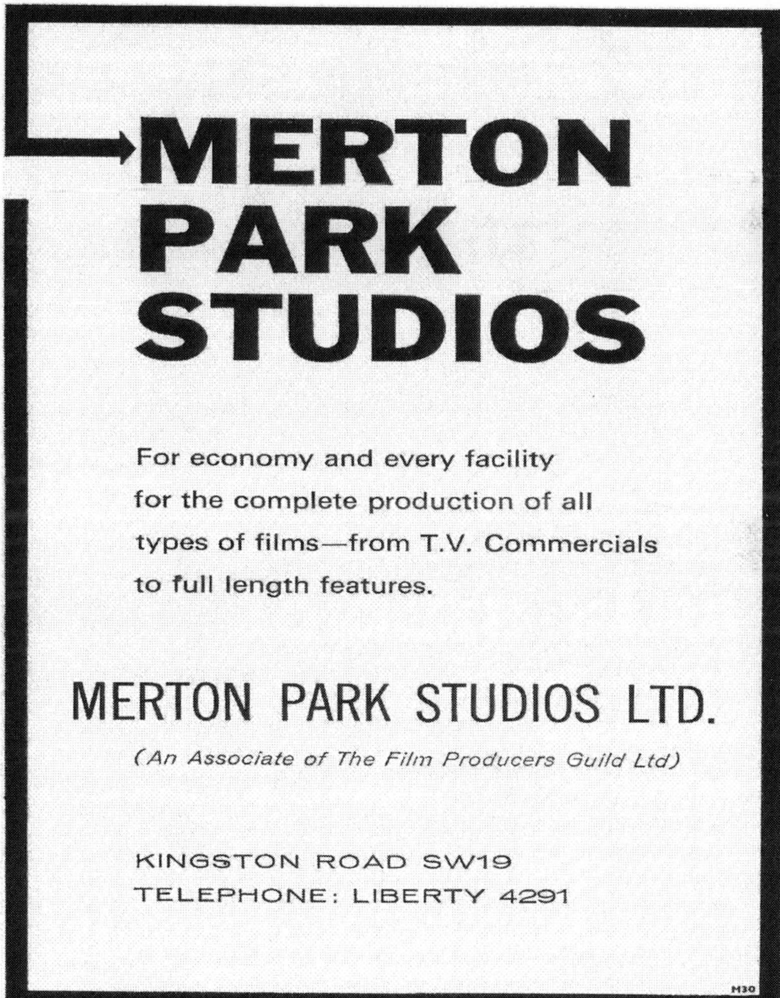

THE CHILDREN'S FILM FOUNDATION

The foundation began in 1951, supported by Lord Rank, and was subsidised by the Eady Levy, a tax on box-office receipts. The idea was to produce films made for children to be shown at Saturday morning picture shows and in schools. Quite often these were in the form of serials to be shown over several consecutive weeks.

Several of these films/series were made at Merton Park studios and a few of the child actors in them were to go on to become well-known adult actors. At Merton Park the child actors included David Hemmings, Michael Crawford, Richard O'Sullivan and Keith Chegwin.

In fact, the very first film made by the CFF was John of the Fair (1952) which was made at Merton Park and which shared a Silver Gondola award at the Venice Film Festival.

The CFF had been preceded by Children's Entertainment Films (CEF) which began in 1947, and before that the Children's Film Department (CFD) which began in 1944.

Very few of these films have been made available on DVD or in any other form, and one, Trouble at Townsend (1946) starring Petula Clark, may or may not be a CFD film, depending on the sources consulted. Strangely, two of the films have been made available on German DVDs, but not British ones: Five Clues to Fortune and Mystery in the Mine.

The list of children's films/series made at Merton Park, including non-CFF ones, is as follows:

JEAN'S PLAN (1946)

Directed by AC Hammond

Screenplay by JO Thomas

Produced by Frank A Hoare

Starring: Billie Brooks, Gerald Case, Vivian Pickles

In his book The Children's Film Foundation Robert Shail briefly outlines the plot as 'the heroine is mainly concerned with thwarting jewel thieves.'

Notes: the following year Billie Brooks starred with a young Anthony Newley in The Adventures of Dusty Bates (1947). Vivian Pickles, who plays the eponymous Jean (her first film) went on to appear in many high-profile productions, including Sunday Bloody Sunday (1971) with Peter Finch and Glenda Jackson and O Lucky Man! (1973) with Malcolm McDowell.

THE SECRET TUNNEL (1947)

Directed by William C Hammond

Screenplay by William C Hammond (based on the book by Mary Cathcart Borer)

Produced by Frank A Hoare

Starring: Tony Wager, Ivor Bowyer, Murray Matheson

Roger Henderson (Wager) and his father live in a grand country house full of antiques and paintings. When a Rembrandt is stolen Roger finds a secret tunnel from the house that he believes may have been used by the thieves and decides to investigate.

Notes: the previous year Tony Wager had appeared as young Pip in David Lean's Great Expectations (1946) with John Mills.

CIRCUS BOY (1947)

Directed by Cecil Musk

Screenplay by Cecil Musk and Mary Cathcart Borer (based on the book by Patita Nicholson)

Produced by Frank A Hoare

Starring: James Kenney, Florence Stephenson, George Stephenson

Michael Scott (Kenney) fails to win the school swimming event and loses confidence in himself so his mother, who previously worked in a circus, persuades him to work in the big top to regain his confidence.

Notes: the circus scenes were filmed at Bertram Mills' circus. Four years later James Kenney was to appear in Captain Horatio Hornblower (1951) with Gregory Peck.

TRAPPED BY THE TERROR (1949)

Directed by Cecil Musk

Screenplay by Mary Cathcart Borer and Sherard Powell (based on a story by Ion Grundy)

Produced by Frank A Hoare

Starring: James Kenney, Colin Simpson, Valerie Carton

Set in the French Revolution, it tells the story of an exiled count who goes back to France to rescue his family.

Notes: the cast includes Martin Benson, who went on to appear in The King and I (1956) with Yul Brynner, Goldfinger (1964) and The Omen (1976).

JOHN OF THE FAIR (1952)

Directed by Michael McCarthy

Screenplay by Michael McCarthy

Produced by Frank A Hoare

Starring: John Charlesworth, Arthur Young, Richard George

Set in 18th century England, it tells the story of John Claydon (Charlesworth) who, although brought up by a seller of herbal remedies, is actually a baronet. A wicked uncle has snatched his rightful position and tries to get rid of him. Robert Shail, author of the book The Children's Film Foundation, describes the film as a 'handsome affair, that skilfully disguises its low budget'

Notes: John Charlesworth had appeared in A Christmas Carol (1951) with Alastair Sim. Cast member Hilda Barry appeared the year after this in one of Merton Park's Scotland Yard episodes, The Drayton Case (1953), and the following decade in Ken Loach's Poor Cow (1967) with Carol White and Terence Stamp.

THE SECRET CAVE (1953)

Directed by John Durst

Screenplay by Joe Mendoza (based on the novel by Thomas Hardy)

Produced by Frank A Hoare

Starring: David Coote, Nick Edmett, Susan Ford

Two boys find an underground river hidden in a cave and divert its course which has serious repercussions in the outside world.

Notes: the cast includes Johnny Morris who became well-known to many children through his TV series Animal Magic (1962–1983).

RAIDERS OF THE RIVER (1955)

Directed by John Haggarty

Screenplay by Robert Martin

Produced by Frank A Hoare

Starring: Richard O'Sullivan, Jenny Jones, Jack McGowran

This was the first of the adventure serials produced by the CFF with eight fifteen-minute episodes. The series has not been released on DVD and no plot details have been published, save from the barest outline that a group of children foil some bank robbers.

Notes: Richard O'Sullivan, who was just ten years old when he starred in this, became a household name in the 1970s through popular TV sitcoms Man About the House and Robin's Nest.

FIVE CLUES TO FORTUNE (aka The Treasure of Woburn Abbey – 1956)

Directed by Joe Mendoza

Screenplay by Joe Mendoza (from a story by Geoffrey Bond)

Produced by Frank A Hoare

Starring: John Rogers, Roberta Paterson, David Hemmings

This was another serial of eight fifteen-minute parts and started with a flashback to the dissolution of the monasteries and some treasure which an abbot hides in a monastery wall before he is taken away by the King's men.

We then see some modern-day children playing in the ruins and discovering clues to the treasure. Naturally, there are some disreputable adults who try to get the fortune for themselves.

Notes: David Hemmings was to go onto considerable success as an adult actor, starring in the iconic sixties film Blow Up (1966) as well as Camelot (1967) and Barbarella (1968) amongst many others.

BLOW YOUR OWN TRUMPET (1957)

Directed by Cecil Musk

Screenplay by Mary Cathcart Borer

Produced by Cecil Musk

Starring: Michael Crawford, Peter Butterworth, Gillian Harrison

Young Jim Fenn (Crawford) wants to play cornet in his local brass band but comes from a poor family who can't afford to buy him an instrument. He also has a rival for the job, the better-off and rather sneaky Tony Holroyd (Martyn Shields).

Notes: Michael Crawford was fourteen when this was made, his second screen role. Within a few years he was starring in swinging 60s film The Knack, and How to Get It (1965) with Rita Tushingham and Ray Brooks and in the 70s took on his most famous role – Frank Spencer in TV comedy series Some Mothers Do 'ave 'em.

This is not on DVD but there is an eight-minute excerpt on YouTube.

MYSTERY IN THE MINE (1959)

Directed by James Hill (Born Free, Giuseppina)

Screenplay by Dallas Bower, James Hill (based on the story by Peter Ling)

Produced by Frank A Hoare

Starring: Ingrid Cardon, Stewart Guidotti, Howard Green, Peter Copley

This was another eight-part serial. Young Tom (Guidotti) goes to stay with his tomboy cousin Jane (Cardon) at the Cornish coast for a couple of weeks and while there discovers some strange goings on. A local scientist, Tom Abbott (Copley) is in league with a criminal who is helping him to sell a rare element they have found down an old mine. Abbott's young assistant, Ray, helps the children bring the two to justice.

Lots of action and outside filming, with a cliff-hanger at the end of each fifteen-minute episode.

Locations: no Merton Park locations, but plenty of outside filming at coast and in countryside.

Notes: Ingrid Cardon was in another Merton Park production that same year, Horrors of the Black Museum (1959).

A few years later, Peter Copley was in the Beatles' second film, Help! (1965).

FOUR WIND ISLAND (1961)

Directed by David Villiers

Screenplay by David Villiers (based on the novel by Vega Stewart)

Produced by Frank A Hoare

Starring: Mandy Harper, Annette Robinson, Ian Gregory, John Pike

Sadly, this title has not been released on DVD and there do not appear to be any synopses available. In his book The Children's Film Foundation, Robert Shail briefly mentions that the plot involves the children finding hidden treasure.

Locations: according to the IMDb the outside filming was done in the Isles of Scilly.

Notes: A couple of years after this film was made Mandy Harper appeared with Susan George in Swallows and Amazons (1963). The year after that, Ian Gregory appeared in quirky cult British film Gonks Go Beat (1964).

EGGHEAD'S ROBOT (1970)

Directed by: Milo Lewis

Screenplay by Leif Saxon

Produced by Cecil Musk

Starring: Keith Chegwin, Roy Kinnear, Patricia Routledge, Richard Wattis

One of the last films made at Merton Park, this was an hour-long comedy caper for the Children's Film Foundation.

Keith Chegwin plays Paul 'Egghead' Wentworth, who builds a robot (played by his brother, Jeffrey Chegwin) which plays cricket and helps in the garden to comic effect.

The character actors, especially Roy Kinnear, make up for a fairly weak script and this would probably have been an adequate kids' film in 1970.

Locations: John Innes Park (in Merton Park) used, also, at the beginning, two of the children are seen cycling along Woodside in Wimbledon.

Notes: A year after this, Keith Chegwin played Fleance in Roman Polanski's controversial film of Macbeth. Also, the Director of Cinematography was one John Coquillon who, also in the following year, was fulfilling the same role on Sam Peckinpah's notorious Straw Dogs!

Keith Chegwin played the Egghead character again in a follow-up film for the Children's Film Foundation, The Troublesome Double (1971) – see below.

THE TROUBLESOME DOUBLE (1971)

Directed by Milo Lewis

Screenplay by Leif Saxon

Produced by Cecil Musk

Starring: Keith Chegwin, Julie Collins, Tracey Collins, Richard Wattis, Josephine Tewson

Keith Chegwin again plays boy inventor Egghead Wentworth, who this time invents a robot double of his sister Elspeth in order to help her win a swimming competition.

Unlike Egghead's Robot, this film has not been released on DVD. There is however a short clip on YouTube.

Locations: there is no record of where the outside filming, such as that of the open-air swimming pool was done, but studio work was at Merton Park.

Notes: Josephine Tewson, who plays Egghead's mother, Mrs Wentworth, went on to appear in TV sitcom Keeping Up Appearances (1990–95) with Patricia Routledge, who had played Egghead's mother in Egghead's Robot (1970).

ANGLO–AMALGAMATED

This British film production company was started in 1945 by Nat Cohen and Stuart Levy and produced many of the films made at Merton Park, including Wide Boy (1952), Horrors of the Black Museum (1959) and The Criminal (1960) as well as all the Edgar Wallace, Scales of Justice and Scotland Yard series.

The company also produced films made at other studios including all the Carry on series up until 1966, starting with Carry on Sergeant (1958) and other high-profile films such as Billy Liar (1963), Darling (1965) and Poor Cow (1967). It also made the controversial Peeping Tom (1960) directed by Michael Powell.

It lasted almost to the end of the time Merton Park studios existed, being taken over by EMI in 1969.

The company had a surprisingly large global reach. An advertisement from 1959 lists over forty countries in which Anglo's films were distributed. Apart from the expected English-speaking countries such as USA, Canada, Australia etc. they also went to USSR, Japan, Iraq, Thailand, and most European countries. The films made at Merton Park therefore were seen all over the world and many were very successful. A 1956 advertisement proudly announces that Confession (starring Sydney Chaplin, and made at Merton Park) 'is now showing in six Paris cinemas! Soon: Wellington, Helsinki, Rome, Berlin, etc.'

The output was pretty phenomenal too. In 1960 Merton Park made three Edgar Wallace films, three Scotland Yard films and four feature films. In 1961 they made nine Edgar Wallace, six Scotland Yard and one feature film, quite apart from what Anglo were making at other studios.

In his book Encyclopaedia of British Film Brian McFarlane says 'A good deal of the history of British filmmaking in the '50s and '60s is encapsulated in the A-A enterprise.'

THE SCOTLAND YARD SERIES (1953–1961)

The stories in this series were all apparently based on true-life crimes taken from the annals of Scotland Yard.

Each episode is introduced by crime writer Edgar Lustgarten, who, in almost every account written of him ever since is described as 'lugubrious'. It is not often noted though how inappropriate his surname is considering his role. The literal translation of Lustgarten is 'pleasure garden'.

At the start of each episode Lustgarten sits at his desk or sometimes gets up to pour himself a drink whilst going over the details of the case about to be shown. Rather than being lugubrious he seems to rather savour the details of other people's misfortunes, occasionally adding in a wry remark regarding the eventual fate of the perpetrator.

The camera will sometimes leave the action mid-episode and return to Lustgarten for a comment or two and then the episode will end with him summing up the case.

The first few episodes of the series were written and directed by Ken Hughes who went on to direct big budget films with Hollywood stars such as Alec Guinness, Richard Harris, Peter Finch, Dick Van Dyke, James Mason, etc.

In fact the first episode of the series, The Drayton Case (1953) was only the second film he had directed, the first being Wide Boy (1952) starring Sydney Tafler, which was also made at Merton Park.

At around thirty minutes each, these film shorts were originally made as supporting features for cinema but ended up on TV both in Britain and the USA.

Over its eight-year run it used several directors and many actors who later became much better known.

Local note: At the beginning of each episode the camera enters the records office of Scotland Yard where, displayed on the shelves, are files containing case histories each with the name of the case on the spine. In some introductions one of these shows the name of Neville Heath, the notorious double murderer from the 1940s who was to feature in the Chamber of Horrors at Madame Tussauds. Although Heath doesn't appear in any of the Scotland Yard episodes it may not be generally known that he went to school (Rutlish) just a few hundred yards from Merton Park studios in Kingston Road, Merton. He was hanged in 1946, just seven years before the Scotland Yard series began.

THE DRAYTON CASE (1953)

Directed by Ken Hughes (Cromwell, Chitty Chitty Bang Bang, The Trials of Oscar Wilde)

Produced by Alec C Snowden

Screenplay by Ken Hughes

Starring: Victor Platt, Hilda Barry, John Le Mesurier

The dead body of a woman is found on a wartime bomb site by workmen and reported to police. Rather than simply assume the woman was a victim of the bomb they have to investigate and after painstaking enquiries and a pathologist's report suspect murder.

Among the people questioned is the woman's estranged husband (Drayton) who denies murder and even claims that after they split up he tried to help her financially.

The investigating officer, Divisional Superintendent Henley (Le Mesurier) has his suspicions though and pursues the case.

A good little police procedural which begins with Edgar Lustgarten asking the viewer 'Have you ever committed a murder?' and going on to enquire what you would do with the body if you had.

It raises the interesting point of how seemingly simple it would have been to dispose of a murdered body at a time when London was full of the corpses of bomb victims.

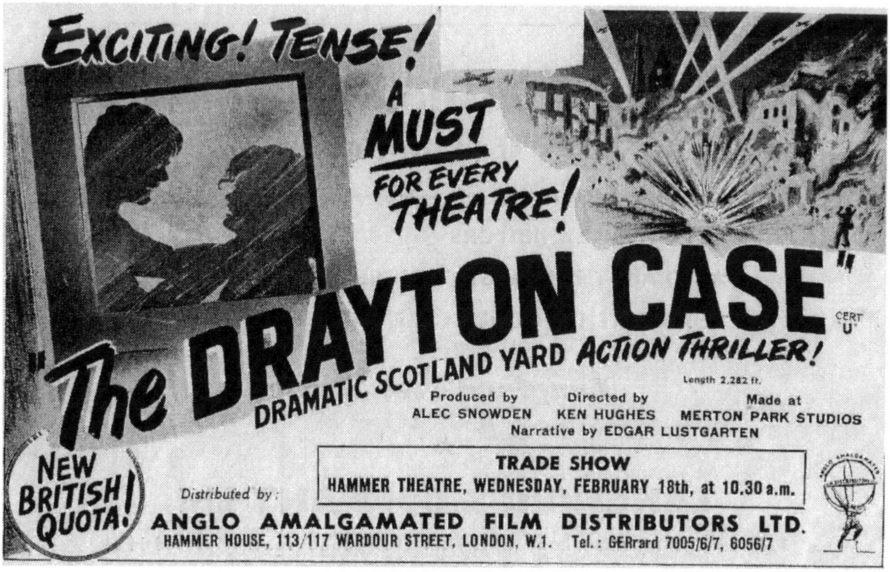

Locations: No obvious Merton Park locations, but this episode was mainly studio-based anyway.

Notes: John Le Mesurier was already over forty when he appeared in this. He had been acting for fifteen years and it would be a further fifteen years before he took on his best-known role as Sergeant Wilson in the Dad's Army TV comedy series.

THE MISSING MAN (1953)

Directed by Ken Hughes

Produced by Alec C Snowden

Screenplay by Ken Hughes

Starring: Tristan Rawson, Evelyn Moore, Axel Moller

A retired vicar and his wife go to London to visit their son and are told that he has gone to Paris. They are perplexed by this as he hadn't told them, and as the days and weeks pass they suspect that there is something seriously wrong. Then the wife has a vivid dream in which she sees her son at a deserted farm and she awakes believing she has had a premonition of his murder.

The vicar goes to Paris in pursuit of his son and eventually the police are involved in the hunt for him which leads them to ... a deserted farm.

Locations: some outside shooting but no obvious Merton Park locations used.

Notes: when a police list of missing persons is shown it includes somebody with the unusual name of John Oldknow, which just happens to be the name of one of the film's production assistants!

THE CANDLELIGHT MURDER (1953)

Directed by Ken Hughes

Produced by Alec C Snowden

Screenplay by Ken Hughes

Starring: Gerald Case, Jack Lambert, Robert Cawdron

A dead body is found under a bridge in shallow water and the face has been badly damaged, possibly deliberately, the police suspect, to prevent identification. They think that the body might be that of local eccentric 'Mad' Thomas who had gone missing a couple of days previously. The body, however, is judged to have been there for about eleven days.

As they make their enquiries they find that not all they thought about the remote dwelling of 'Mad' Thomas is quite as it seems.

Locations: No Merton Park locations.

Notes: Gerald Case had appeared in the film of Henry V with Laurence Olivier in 1944 and in 1980 appeared in the Elephant Man alongside John Hurt, Anthony Hopkins and John Gielgud.

THE BLAZING CARAVAN (1953)

Directed by Ken Hughes

Produced by Alec C Snowden

Screenplay by Ken Hughes

Starring: Alexander Gauge, Edgar Driver, Alan Robinson, Betty Carter

A taxidermist (Mr Buxton, played by Gauge) wins £30,000 on the football pools ('I'm a millionaire!' he exclaims, and by 2019 £30,000 would be worth almost a million) and is then found murdered. His body is disposed of in a caravan fire.

The police investigate and manage to find the killer.

Locations: When one of the characters goes to the bank it is situated at the corner of Rothesay Avenue, which was just a few hundred yards from the studios. The shops in adjacent Kingston Road can be seen in the background.

Notes: When Mr Buxton has his pools win he offers to buy all his friends and acquaintances a drink at the 'Leather Bottle' pub. Although this scene is filmed in the studio, the real Leather Bottle pub, a favourite with actors and crew, was just yards from Merton Park studios.

THE DARK STAIRWAY (1954)

Directed by Ken Hughes

Produced by Alec C Snowden

Screenplay by Ken Hughes

Starring: Russell Napier, Vincent Ball, George Manship, Edwin Richfield

A man named Harry Carpenter is murdered on the eponymous 'dark stairway' and a female neighbour sees the body and a man with dark glasses bending over it. She screams, the police are called and the man in dark glasses, who is blind, is arrested but refuses to talk.

In the meantime it emerges that the dead man had been a criminal who informed on one of his accomplices, named Joe Lloyd (Richfield) who has just been released from prison. So now he too is a suspect, but the police, led by Inspector Harmer (Napier) have trouble finding him.A good little film noir with a nice twist at the end.

Locations: no obvious Merton Park exteriors.

Notes: this was the first of many Scotland Yard episodes to feature Russell Napier as a police inspector, most often as Inspector or Superintendent Duggan, though in this he is Inspector Harmer.

LATE NIGHT FINAL (1954)

Directed by Montgomery Tully (Electronic Monster, Strange Awakening, Boys in Brown)

Produced by Alec C Snowden

Screenplay by Montgomery Tully, Gaston Charpentier

Starring: Colin Tapley, Terry Yorke, Frank Forsyth, Stanley Van Beers

Newspaper seller Joe Burrage (Van Beers) is the only witness to a robbery in the docklands area, but when the police want to speak to him he has mysteriously disappeared.

Unusually for the time, the plot involves the smuggling of cocaine.

Locations: no obvious Merton Park locations.

Notes: Margot Bryant, who had a small part as a landlady, later became well-known playing the part of Minnie Caldwell in Coronation Street.

Director Montgomery Tully went on to direct many films at Merton Park including Counterfeit Plan (1956), Electronic Monster (1958) and Strange Awakening (aka Female Fiends, 1958).

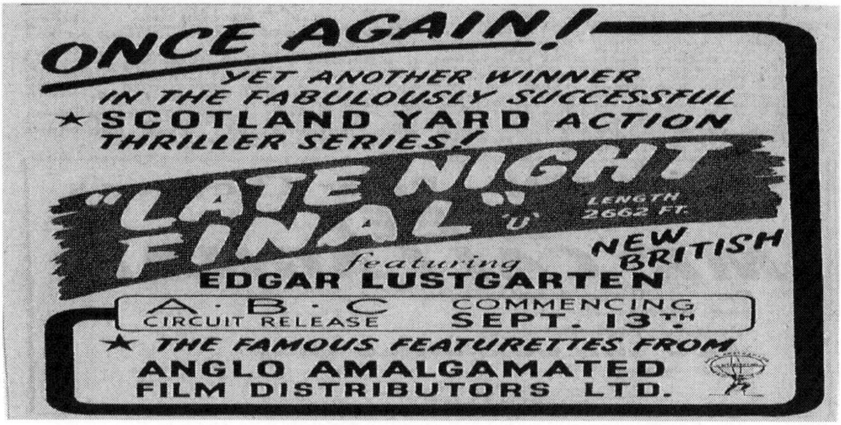

FATAL JOURNEY (1954)

Directed by Paul Dickson (as Paul Gherzo)

Produced by Alec C Snowden

Screenplay by James Eastwood

Starring: Gordon Bell, Edward Forsyth, Julian Somers, Jack Melford, Jane Welch

A man on a train (Somers) seems to have lost his memory and is taken to hospital. The police identify him as 'Goff' but he apparently still remembers nothing about himself.

In the meantime, on returning from work a man named Preston (Melford) discovers his wife (Welch) lying on the floor having been attacked by an intruder. A gypsy (Peter Halliday) is suspected of the attack and robbery. The gypsy eventually admits the robbery but denies attacking the woman, who later dies. The police then attempt to link Goff to the murder.

An interesting story in which new bits of information are revealed as the plot progresses.

Locations: It is possible that the station shown when Goff catches the train is Merton Park.

Notes: this was Peter Halliday's first screen role and he went on to have a lifelong career in acting, mainly on TV.

Director Paul Dickson went on to a successful career in TV series such as the Avengers, Jason King, and Department S. It's possible that he used the pseudonym for this job as he was simultaneously working on a TV series named Calling Scotland Yard and using his real name may have caused confusion.

THE STRANGE CASE OF BLONDIE (1954)

Directed by Ken Hughes

Produced by Alec C Snowden

Screenplay by Ken Hughes, Basil Francis

Starring: Russell Napier, Derek Aylward, Lee Sinclaire, Ian Wilson

A series of break-ins has occurred and the police suspect a young woman they nickname Blondie. In one of the break-ins though the perpetrator is disturbed and attacks the householder, who dies.

A young blonde woman has been carrying out house-to-house opinion polls and, the police believe, using that as a pretext to 'case the joint' prior to a robbery.

Meanwhile, a man with a moustache has been trying to sell some of the stolen goods to a pawnbroker. Is it 'Blondie' in disguise?

Russell Napier plays the investigating detective, Inspector Harmer, and Derek Aylward is his would-be wisecracking assistant, Langham, whose humour Harmer tries to rein in.

A good story with quite a bit of colour due to some theatre scenes and a fair bit of location shooting.

Locations: several Merton Park/Wimbledon locations used, including Kingston Road, near the studios and Wimbledon Theatre. We also see the 77a bus, with Blondie on board, leaving the West End and arriving outside the old Co-op shop in Kingston Road.

Notes: The location of 'The Comedy Theatre, Wimbledon' is mentioned and an exterior shot of the stage door at the real Wimbledon Theatre is shown. It's possible that some of the interior theatre scenes were shot inside Wimbledon theatre too.

Despite having a sizeable role in this film, actor Lee Sinclaire doesn't seem to have appeared in anything before or since.

This was the last episode in the series to be written and directed by Ken Hughes.

THE SILENT WITNESS (1953)

Directed by Montgomery Tully

Produced by Alec C Snowden

Screenplay by James Eastwood

Starring: Kenneth Henry, Frank Forsyth, Ivan Craig, Namana Michael

A man named Stafford (Craig) phones the police to say he has killed his wife, claiming it was an accident which happened when they were having an argument.

However, there seems to be more to this than first appears and the police begin to uncover more about the peculiar circumstances surrounding the case while the man is held in custody.

Detective Forbes (Forsyth) discovers there was a witness to the murder – but why didn't they come forward?

Locations: no obvious Merton Park locations.

Notes: well-known comedy actress Rita Webb plays a small part as a greengrocer. This was the first of several appearances in this series for her.

Although filmed in 1953 this wasn't shown until 1954, after The Strange Case of Blondie (1954).

PASSENGER TO TOKYO (1954)

Directed by Ken Hughes

Produced by Alec C Snowden

Screenplay by James Eastwood

Starring: Kenneth Henry, Ken Marshall, Peter Penn, Dorothy Bramhall

A rather exotic episode for the series, taking in locations as far afield as Tokyo and Cape Town (using stock footage and studio sets of course!)

Arriving in Tokyo a man is shocked when customs men open a trunk, supposedly belonging to him, which contains the dismembered body of a woman.

He pleads ignorance of the trunk and its contents and it is later confirmed that the trunk did not belong to him. The police, led by Superintendent Ross (Henry) then begin extensive investigations to find who sent the trunk, and also who the dead woman was.

Quite a complex plot to fit into half an hour with lots of twists and turns and different characters, but a change from the more parochial locations of many of the other episodes in this series.

Locations: no Merton Park locations.

Notes: Kenneth Henry also played a police inspector in Merton Park film Terror Ship that same year, 1954.Totti Truman Taylor, who has a small part as a headmistress in this film appeared in a later film directed by Ken Hughes – Chitty Chitty Bang Bang (1968), as The Duchess.

NIGHT PLANE TO AMSTERDAM (1954)

Directed by Ken Hughes

Produced by Alec C Snowden

Screenplay by James Eastwood

Starring: Gerald Case, Shay Gorman, Selma Vaz Dias, Derek Sydney

A criminal by the name of Bosker (Sydney) is interrupted when stealing a necklace and murders the maid who walked in on him.

The police, led by Inspector Carron (Case) realise that someone has been fencing the stolen goods which necessitates the inspector flying to Amsterdam to follow the trail.

Locations: no exterior shooting in Merton Park.

Notes: Gerald Case had played the same character (Superintendent Carron) in a previous Scotland Yard episode, The Candlelight Murder.

THE STATELESS MAN (1955)

Directed by Paul Dickson (as Paul Gherzo – The Avengers, Jason King, etc.)

Screenplay by James Eastwood

Produced by Alec C Snowden

Starring: Frank Leighton, Robin Wentworth, Theodore Wilhelm, Tom Clegg, May Hallet

A man named Slavik (Wilhelm) is seen by a policemen running in panic down a docklands street. He runs away before the policeman can stop him.

Meanwhile, the dead body of a young woman is found in the bedroom of a nearby boarding house and a letter from Slavik is found in the room.

The police manage to connect the running man with the murder but he pleads innocence and the investigation widens to the landlady and her son.

A good thriller with some excellent performances, particularly May Hallet as the short-tempered and matriarchal landlady, Mrs Fenton.

Locations: None in Merton Park but some filming in the docklands when it was still a working docks area.

Notes: May Hallet had appeared in prestigious films such as Powell and Pressburger's Black Narcissus (1947) and later in Separate Tables (1958) with Deborah Kerr, David Niven and Rita Hayworth.

Robin Wentworth later became well-known as Arthur Dewhurst in Coronation Street from 1961–69.

THE MYSTERIOUS BULLET (1955)

Directed by Paul Dickson (as Paul Gherzo)

Screenplay by James Eastwood

Produced by Alec C Snowden

Starring: Robert Raglan, John Stuart, John Warwick, Christine Adrian

A man is caught poaching using a gun and as he is being led away by the gamekeeper who caught him, they come across the dead body of the landowner.

The poacher is suspected of the killing but denies it and the police investigate further, questioning the dead man's fiancée and others.

Locations: no Merton Park locations.

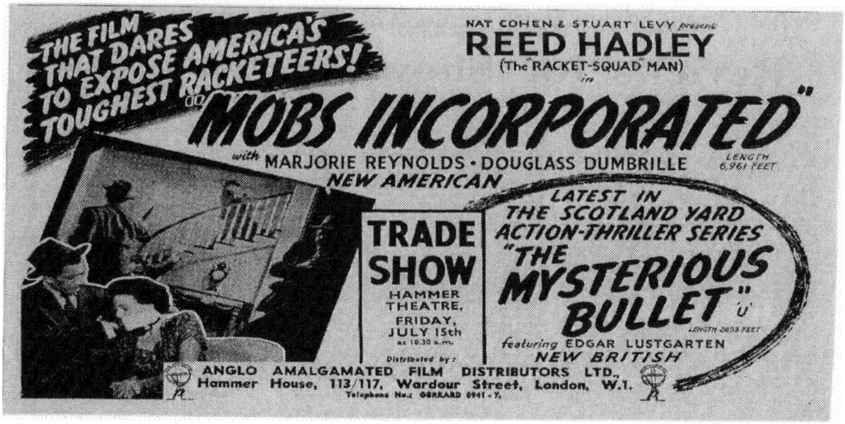

Mysterious Bullet supporting the non-Merton Park film Mobs Incorporated

Notes: the ballistics expert who appears in the film was real-life gun-maker Robert Churchill who had been called as an expert in many famous trials over the years. Edie Martin, who plays a small part in this film had previously appeared in Ealing comedies such as The Man in the White Suit (1951), The Lavender Hill Mob (1951) and The Titfield Thunderbolt (1953).

MURDER ANONYMOUS (1955)

Directed by Ken Hughes

Screenplay by James Eastwood

Produced by Alec C Snowden

Starring: Jill Bennett, Peter Arne, Ewen Solon, Brian O'Higgins

A man is found dead and although there is a gun nearby he has not been shot. It turns out that he has been having an affair with a Mrs Sheldon (Bennett). Could the murderer have been her husband (Arne) who is blind and needs his guide dog wherever he goes? Quite a star-studded cast for this film with Jill Bennett, Vanda Godsell, Arthur Lowe and Peter Arne being experienced actors who were all to go on to greater things.

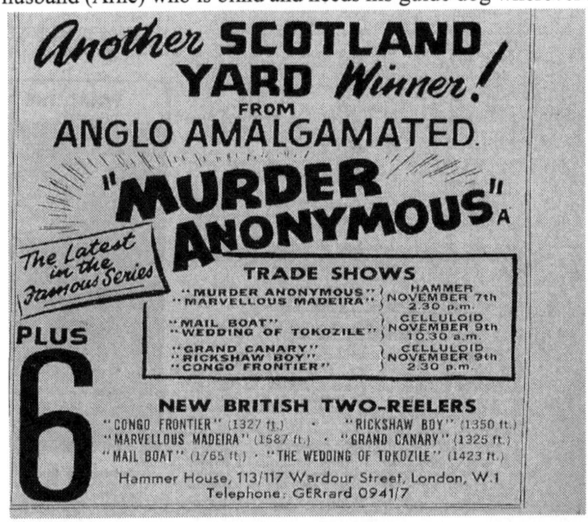

Locations: no obvious Merton Park locations.

Notes: Arthur Lowe plays a small, uncredited part as a fingerprint expert. Jill Bennett had already been in John Huston's Moulin Rouge (1952) and was to go on to be in The Charge of the Light Brigade (1968) and For Your Eyes Only (1981). Peter Arne was to appear in Chitty Chitty Bang Bang (1968) and Straw Dogs (1971).

Well-known real-life judge Travers Christmas Humphries was introduced by Edgar Lustgarten at the beginning of this episode to give his opinion on why miscarriages of justice happen. He was 87 at the time, just a year before he died.

WALL OF DEATH (1955)

Directed by Montgomery Tully

Screenplay by Montgomery Tully and Judith Warden

Produced by Alec C Snowden

Starring: Cyril Chamberlain, Vernon Greeve, Vanda Godsell, Ferdy Mayne

A circus 'Wall of Death' rider is killed when his motorbike loses power during a performance and his petrol tank explodes. Police find that someone had put sugar in his petrol tank which caused it to seize up.

His wife, Nina Hartier (Godsell) is questioned and it is found that she is very close to trapeze artist Rudy Schmidt (Mayne). Police wonder if it could have been him who tampered with the bike in order to get rid of his love rival.

A reasonable episode enhanced by the unusual setting and some strong performances.

Locations: no Merton Park locations. The circus scenes were filmed at Kursaal amusement park, Southend-on-sea.

Notes: Cyril Chamberlain who played Inspector Harris featured in many of the Carry On films, including the very first, Carry On Sergeant in 1958.

THE CASE OF THE RIVER MORGUE (1956)

Directed by Montgomery Tully

Screenplay by Montgomery Tully

Produced by Alec C Snowden

Starring: Hugh Moxey, Gordon Needham, Jane Welsh, Charles Mortimer

A mortuary attendant opens a drawer expecting to find the body he needs to examine but finds it has been stolen! Even more strangely, after the police have been called in to investigate, the body mysteriously reappears in the drawer the next day. But is it the same body?

Police are initially baffled, but after some painstaking detective work finally get to the bottom of it and determine whether or not the man's death was accidental. Their investigations take them as far afield as Paris.

An unusual story, and another episode that allows the scene to shift from the UK to a more exotic location.

Locations: the police are seen in a car outside the studio with the Merton Park Parade shops visible in the background.

Notes: Andre Maranne, a French actor who plays a gendarme in this film later appeared in five of the Pink Panther films.

DESTINATION DEATH (1956)

Directed by Montgomery Tully

Screenplay by Colin S Reid

Produced by Alec C Snowden

Starring: Russell Napier, Arthur Gomez, Melissa Stribling

A man is found dead in London Airport's departure lounge. The police find he has a bottle which contained poisoned brandy, and also a signed photo from a female nightclub singer.

They trace the nightclub singer, Kara (Colette Wilde) to Lisbon, Portugal, but she denies all knowledge of the dead man whom the police have now identified, though by a lucky chance they now discover Kara's involvement in a currency smuggling ring.

This still leaves them to get to the bottom of the mystery of the dead man – murder or suicide?

Locations: no obvious Merton Park locations, and again, the action shifts outside the UK, even though in reality the actors stayed in Merton Park!

Notes: This episode marks the first appearance of Inspector Duggan (Napier), though Napier had already been in The Dark Stairway (1954) as Inspector Harmer.

PERSON UNKNOWN (1956)

Directed by Montgomery Tully

Screenplay by James Eastwood

Produced by Alec C Snowden

Starring: Russell Napier, Marianne Stone, George Pravda, Edward Cast

A dead body is found at a quarry after an explosion and it belongs to a Polish man by the name of Cusick (Pravda). The police suspect foul play and question his wife (Stone).

On further enquiry they find that the dead man had in fact been a spy and that there is more to the case than meets the eye. The police investigations are once again led by Inspector Duggan (Napier).

Locations: no Merton Park locations, but the quarry, and possibly some other outside locations, were in Amberley, West Sussex.

Notes: George Pravda went on to appear in the Bond film, Thunderball (1965). This Scotland Yard episode was his first English language film.

Marianne Stone had already appeared in John Boulting's Brighton Rock (1948) and later appeared in Stanley Kubrick's Lolita (1962).

THE LONELY HOUSE (1957)

Directed by Montgomery Tully

Screenplay by James Eastwood

Produced by Alec C Snowden

Starring: Russell Napier, Gordon Needham, Frank Forsyth, Bettina Dickson, Totti Truman Taylor

Workmen resurfacing a road find a dead body in the barrel of hot tar they are using. Meanwhile, police are investigating a dating agency whose clients have a suspiciously high mortality rate. Could there be a connection?

The investigation is in the capable hands of Inspector Duggan (Napier) and his sidekick Sergeant Conway (Needham).

Locations: no obvious Merton Park locations.

Notes: Ludovic Kennedy plays a newsreader.

BULLET FROM THE PAST (1957)

Directed by Kenneth Hume (I've Gotta Horse, Cheer The Brave, Hot Ice)

Screenplay by Donovan Winter (uncredited)

Produced by Alec C Snowden

Starring: Ballard Berkeley, Duncan McIntyre, Donovan Winter, Robert Sansom

A housekeeper finds her boss dead on the floor and in his hand is a revolver that has been recently fired. The bullet removed from his head however was not fired by that gun.

Inspector Berkeley (Ballard Berkeley) then has the job of finding who did shoot the victim and has to follow up the meagre clues left at the scene of the crime.

Locations: the story is set in Surrey, so no Merton Park locations.

Notes: Although an experienced actor Ballard Berkeley was to become far better known a couple of decades later as the dotty major in Fawlty Towers ('papers arrived yet Fawlty?').

The policeman, Sergeant Scott was played by Donovan Winter, who wrote the screenplay.

A young Patrick Newell, who was to play the 'Mother' character in the Avengers, as well as many other roles over a long career, has a small, uncredited part as a postal worker.

INSIDE INFORMATION (1957)

Directed by Montgomery Tully

Screenplay by James Eastwood

Produced by Alec C Snowden

Starring: Ronald Adam, Bernard Fox, Basil Henson, Colette Wilde

At a Guy Fawkes night display the body in the bonfire turns out to be that of a real man rather than an effigy.

Inspector Hammond (Adam) investigates but when he enlists the help of a crime reporter he too is murdered.

Locations: one of the suspects lives in a supposedly remote house, but it is in fact at the corner of Camp Road and Westside, Wimbledon Common. West View, Wimbledon is also seen, as is the exterior of Nelson hospital opposite the studios. Merton Park garage, next to the studios is also shown.

Notes: Ronald Adam was a veteran of both world wars and was reputedly shot down by the 'Red Baron' in 1918 before becoming a prisoner of war.

Bernard Fox had a long acting career, appearing in Titanic (1997) and The Mummy (1999).

THE CASE OF THE SMILING WIDOW (1957)

Directed by Montgomery Tully

Screenplay by Gil Saunders

Produced by Alec C Snowden

Starring: Russell Napier, Vernon Greeves. Roger Delgardo, Sylvia Marriot

The housekeeper walks into the kitchen of her employer, art dealer Christopher Nicholls, and finds the dead body of his friend, painter Peter Adams, on the floor with his head in the gas oven. Nicholls claims that Adams had been drinking heavily the night before, but this fact is disputed by the pathologist and the case is investigated by Inspector Duggan (Napier) and his sidekick sergeant (Greeves) who, with information from their driver (Glyn Houston), find that there is more to this than meets the eye.

The 'Smiling Widow' of the title is the name of a valuable painting that Adams had forged many years previously and which had been sold by Nicholls. At one point, Duggan has to travel to Rome for background information on the painting – another example of the series attempting to make an episode more exotic and move out of the small world of South London low-life.

Locations: no Merton Park locations.

Notes: Vernon Greeves had appeared in Laurence Olivier's film of Henry V (1944) and Sylvia Marriott was to go on to play in Bond film Never Say Never Again (1983) and Spielberg's Empire of the Sun (1987).

It is strange to see Glyn Houston playing the small part of the police driver as he had already been in several films, including two at Merton Park, Wide Boy (1952), and The Great Game (1953) in which he played a leading role.

Perhaps there should have been a Scotland Yard episode entitled The Case of the Missing Author, as the screenwriter Gil Saunders (as with one or two other Merton Park screenwriters) never seemed to write anything before or since.

THE MAIL VAN MURDER (1957)

Directed by John Knight (The Avengers, Armchair Theatre)

Screenplay by James Eastwood

Produced by Alec C Snowden

Starring: Hy Hazell, Dennis Castle, Gordon Needham, Robert Reardon

Police find the dead body of a Royal Mail worker, then the scene changes to a man named Jack Tanner (Reardon) being released from prison and looking up some of his accomplices in the mail robbery he alone served time for. They are not pleased to see him and it's not long before he is the next victim of a murder.

Superintendent Hammond (Castle) and Sergeant Wilson (Needham) investigate.

Locations: no Merton Park locations.

Notes: this was the third episode of the series in which writer James Eastwood uses the name Fenton for one of the characters (others were The Stateless Man and Person Unknown).

Jack Howarth has a small, uncredited role as a cleaner but was to become well-known as Albert Tatlock in TV's Coronation Street from 1960–2000. June Cunningham, who also had a small uncredited role was that same year in The Scamp with Richard Attenborough and Big Time Operators with Peter Sellers. In 1959 she was in Merton Park's Horrors of the Black Museum.

John Knight also directed episodes of Merton Park series Scales of Justice and the Edgar Wallace mysteries.

This was the first of several Scotland Yard episodes to include black or Asian characters.

THE TYBURN CASE (1957)

Directed by David Paltenghi (Electronic Monster, Love Match, Keep it Clean)

Screenplay by James Eastwood

Produced by Alec C Snowden

Starring: John Warwick, Gordon Needham, Howard Marion-Crawford, Patricia Marmont

The dead body of a woman is found in the sewers by the underground Tyburn river. Police manage to trace who she was by the clothes she was wearing, but according to some people they question, the woman of that name is still alive.

Locations: no Merton Park locations, and once again, the police inspector is getting on a plane – this time to the Bahamas – as part of the investigation.

Notes: Howard Marion-Crawford later appeared in David Lean's Lawrence of Arabia (1962) and Patricia Marmont had appeared the previous year in Helen of Troy with Stanley Baker and Brigitte Bardot.

THE WHITE CLIFFS MYSTERY (1957)

Directed by Montgomery Tully

Screenplay by James Eastwood

Produced by Alec C Snowden

Starring: Russell Napier, Julian Strange, Alan Robinson

A man's body falls from a train going from Seahaven to Waterloo and the police are called in as it appears that the man, named Matrion, had been strangled. The police, led by Inspector Duggan (Napier), find that Matrion had stayed at a hotel in Seahaven under a false name. Then the body of his secretary is found dead by the cliffs ...

Locations: The junction of Palmerston Road and Kingston Road, Merton, not far from where the studios were based.

Notes: Gillian Vaughan plays a small, uncredited part as a hotel receptionist – her first film) but by the following year was in The Horse's Mouth (1958) with Alec Guinness and Merton Park regular, Michael Gough.

Michael Mellinger who plays the character Josef Armed later appeared in several big-budget films such as Goldfinger (1964), The Bourne Identity (1988) and Gladiator (2000).

NIGHT CROSSING (1957)

Directed by Montgomery Tully

Screenplay by James Eastwood

Produced by Alec C Snowden

Starring: Russell Napier, Julian Strange, John Serret, Andre Maranne

A fisherman finds a woman's body on the beach and reports it to police. At first, they believe it is that of a black woman with marks on her body indicating use of a hypodermic needle and possible drug addiction, but they later discover that it was a white woman who had used some sort of skin colouring.

The investigating officer is Inspector Duggan (Napier) who has to go to Paris to follow up on a lead relating to a club owner named Ricco.

Locations: no Merton Park locations.

Notes: Duggan's sidekick is Sergeant Jason, played by Julian Strange, but in the previous episode, The White Cliffs Mystery Strange played a Sergeant Blunt.

It is odd that as Napier so often played the main detective he did not have a regular sidekick in order to establish the sort of crime duo pairing that dated back to Holmes and Watson and which might have enhanced the identity of the series.

PRINT OF DEATH (1958)

Directed by Montgomery Tully (Man With a Gun, Electronic Monster)

Screenplay by James Eastwood

Produced by Jack Greenwood

Starring: John Warwick, Tim Turner, Phil Brown, Edwin Richfield

Someone has been robbing security vans carrying wages in cash and the fingerprints found indicate it was a man well-known to police who has just been released from jail.

The robberies continue however after it is found that the man is dead. The police investigate and find out the truth which turns out to be rather grisly.

The detective, Inspector Reynolds (Warwick), makes a second appearance, having featured in The Tyburn Case.

For some reason it was decided this time to have an American sidekick for the investigating officer. His name was Kovacs (Brown) and was supposed to be on some sort of exchange trip. Brown later appeared in films such as Star Wars episode IV (1977) and Superman (1978).

Locations: no Merton Park locations, but quite a bit of outside filming in streets, railway sidings etc.

Notes: when Kovacs uses the expression 'mug shot', Inspector Reynolds is unfamiliar with the phrase and has to have it explained to him.

This was Jack Greenwood's first episode as producer, and indeed first job as a producer apart from a documentary short. He went on to produce many films at Merton Park, including The Criminal (1960) featuring Stanley Baker.

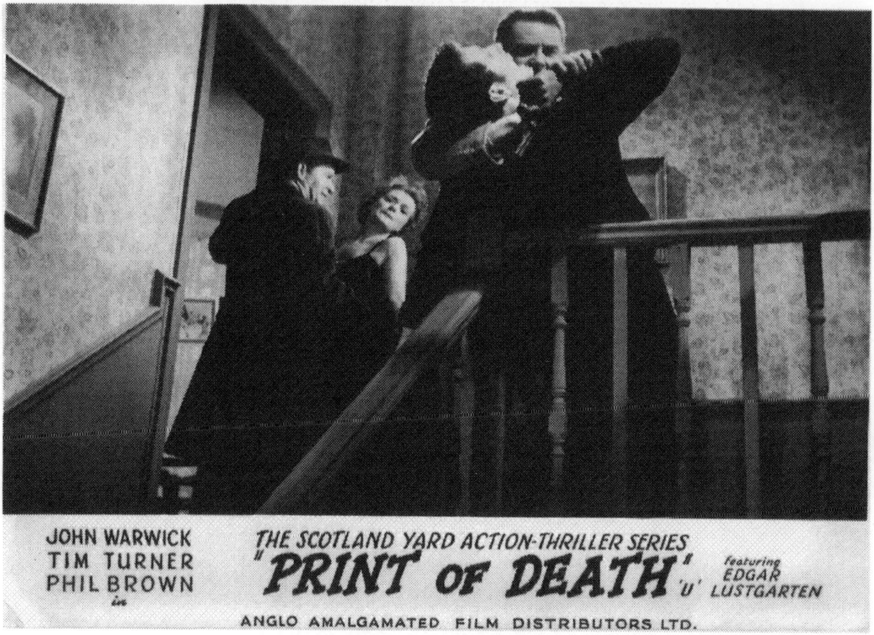

CRIME OF HONOUR (1958)

Directed by Montgomery Tully

Screenplay by James Eastwood

Produced by Jack Greenwood

Starring: Russell Napier, Jean Lodge, Ivan Craig, Julian Strange

A dredger in the Thames Estuary pulls out the dead body of a man which is identified as being that of someone connected with importing wine from Spain. It is also found that the man had been strangled.

Inspector Duggan (Napier) has to travel to Spain to investigate further and we are treated to some flamenco dancing and local colour before he returns by ship and questions the crew about the dead man's similar journey just before he was killed.

Naturally, the story becomes more complex, with the crime of bigamy added to the crime of murder being investigated.

Locations: Church Lane, Merton Park, just across the road from the studios.

Notes: four years previously, Ivan Craig, who plays one of the wine importers, had appeared in Hell Below Zero with Alan Ladd (1954). Gillian Vaughan, who went onto bigger things appeared in another small, uncredited role as she had done in The White Cliffs Mystery.

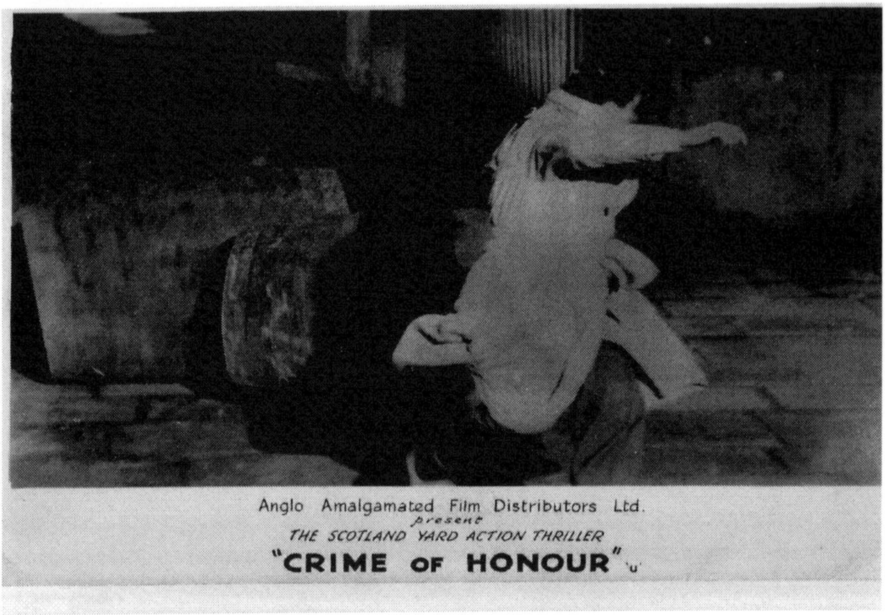

THE CROSS ROAD GALLOWS (1958)

Directed by Montgomery Tully

Screenplay by James Eastwood

Produced by Jack Greenwood

Starring: John Warwick, David Lodge, Tim Turner, Arthur Gomez

A farmer (Gomez) finds a caravan parked on his land, but when he enters it to tell the occupants to leave he finds a young couple who have been murdered after a brutal assault.

Inspector Reynolds (Warwick) investigates and wonders why the farmer is so aggressive and defensive about his property which he will not allow police to search. The farmer's wife then reveals a secret in the attic ...

Locations: a garage in Watery Lane, Merton Park, just opposite the studios.

Notes: David Lodge went on to many TV and film roles, including I'm All right Jack (1959) and Two Way Stretch (1960), both starring Peter Sellers.

THE UNSEEING EYE (1959)

Directed by Geoffrey Muller (Ghost Train Murder, The Witness, The Last Train)

Screenplay by James Eastwood

Produced by Jack Greenwood

Starring: Russell Napier, John Stone, Garard Green, Gordon Bell

A fire is discovered in some unused offices, but there is a dead body there too. Police have trouble identifying the man. The only clue they discover is a false eye which they believe to have been manufactured in the USA.

The investigation is led by Inspector Duggan (Napier) with a new sidekick, Sergeant Nixon (John Stone). As part of the investigation Duggan has to travel to Paris.

Locations: Morden underground station, not far from the studios.

Notes: This was Geoffrey Muller's first directorial role though he had been editor on many other Merton Park productions, including The Dark Man, and Mystery Junction (both 1951) as well as earlier episodes of the Scotland Yard series.

THE GHOST TRAIN MURDER (1959)

Directed by Geoffrey Muller (The Witness, The Last Train)

Screenplay by James Eastwood

Produced by Jack Greenwood

Starring: Russell Napier, Gordon Needham, Jill Ireland

A couple get off the ghost train ride at the funfair and the woman tells the operator she saw the body of a girl lying by the side of the track. It turns out to be that of a Hungarian refugee who had been in trouble with the police for shoplifting.

Inspector Duggan (Napier) investigates with Sergeant Adams (Needham) and they have to determine whether the killer was the young man who had just bought her an engagement ring then threatened her when she saw other men. He, of course, denies murder, but who else could have done it?

Locations: no Merton Park locations.

Notes: Although Gordon Needham had played Inspector Duggan's sidekick in the Lonely House episode he was known then as Sergeant Conway. Needham had also appeared in other previous episodes, each time with a different name! He was Sergeant Stafford in the Case of the River Morgue, Sergeant Wilson in The Mail Van Murder, and Sergeant Hale in The Tyburn Case.

Jill Ireland was married to David McCallum and appeared in several episodes of The Man From Uncle TV series with him, as well as the film Hell Drivers (1957). Her second husband was Charles Bronson and she appeared in several films with him too.

THE DOVER ROAD MYSTERY (1960)

Directed by Gerard Bryant (Rock Around the World, All Square Aft)

Screenplay by James Eastwood

Produced by Jack Greenwood

Starring: Geoffrey Keen, Edward Cast, Leonard Sachs, Jane Rieger

A high-performance car is used in an armed bank robbery during which a member of the staff is shot. Was the owner of the car involved, or should the police believe his story that it was stolen? The crime is investigated by Superintendent Graham (Keen) and his sidekick, Sergeant Webster (Cast).

This episode makes use of some different outdoor locations, e.g. a golf course and a car racing track, without resorting to stock film to add a bit of colour.

Locations: the bank that is robbed is at the junction of Rothesay Avenue and Kingston Road, Merton, the same location as the bank in the Blazing Caravan episode.

Notes: Between 1977 and 1987 Geoffrey Keen appeared in half a dozen Bond films, usually as Minister of Defence, starting with The Spy Who Loved Me and ending with The Living Daylights. Coincidentally, Leonard Sachs also appeared in Thunderball (1965).

Before going into directing, Gerard Bryant had been a production manager on Boulting's film of Graham Greene's Brighton Rock starring Richard Attenborough and had also written for several films between the 1940s and 1970s.

THE LAST TRAIN (1960)

Directed by Geoffrey Muller (Ghost Train Murder, The Witness, The Unseeing Eye)

Screenplay by James Eastwood

Produced by Jack Greenwood

Starring: Russell Napier, Norman Johns, Lisa Daniely, Howard Pays

A guard finds the dead body of a man on a tube train. He has been shot and has a gun in his hand, but there is also a bullet lodged in the wall of the train carriage. Was it suicide or murder, with the murderer planting the gun is his hand?

Yet another case for Superintendent Duggan (Napier) with yet another new sidekick, Sergeant Adams (Johns).

Locations: police call at a house in Sandbourne Avenue, Merton Park.

Notes: the tube station at which the man's body is found has the name Oxley Green, a fictitious station, but the actual station used is believed to be the now disused Aldwych, which by the time of filming was closed at weekends and would therefore have been easier to use than South Wimbledon station which was near the studios. It is not clear though why the sign did not show South Wimbledon rather than Oxley Green as we are told that the dead man lived in SW19, a short walk from the station.

Hilda Barry, who plays a small part in this film, had already appeared in two Merton Park films, The Hypnotist (1957) and Horrors of the Black Museum (1959) as well as many TV series. Norman Johns, still a young man when he appeared in this film, was to die tragically young just three years later.

EVIDENCE IN CONCRETE (1961)

Directed by Gordon Hales (Return to Sender, Undesirable Neighbour)

Screenplay by James Eastwood

Produced by Jack Greenwood

Starring: Russell Napier, Howard Pays, Peter Welch, Jill Hyem

A young woman's body is found by the side of the road and at first police suspect a hit and run accident, but then notice that although she has blood on her clothes there is none on the ground, indicating the body had been moved after death. Simultaneously, a lorry load of whiskey has been stolen. Is there a connection?

Locations: no Merton Park locations used.

Notes: Howard Pays is Duggan's sidekick this time but is called Sergeant Adams. In his last appearance as Duggan's assistant he was called Sergeant Davy. In the early 1960s he set up a highly successful theatrical agency and gave up his acting career.

The newsreader is played by real-life newsreader Kenneth Kendall.

THE SILENT WEAPON (1961)

Directed by Peter Duffell (Scales of Justice, Edgar Wallace series, Avengers)

Screenplay by James Eastwood

Produced by Jack Greenwood

Starring: Geoffrey Keen, Stanley Morgan, Michael Nightingale, Norma Parnell

Two men are out riding one morning when a shot is heard and one of the men falls from his horse. It is later discovered that he had not been shot but had received a heavy blow to the head, not caused when he fell from the horse. His young riding companion is questioned by the police who know that he has a criminal record for theft.

Apart from finding who killed the man, the police led by Superintendent Carter (Keen) have to find the murder weapon as there was not one at the scene of the death. It turns out to be something very unexpected ...

Locations: several Merton Park locations, including Watery Lane and Nelson hospital, directly opposite the studio, and Morden underground station. There is also footage of a greyhound racing stadium but it is not clear if this was the old Wimbledon dog track.

Notes: when Geoffrey Keen last played a police inspector in this series he was Superintendent Graham in the Dover Road Mystery. Stanley Morgan, who played Detective Sergeant Dobbs was to appear in many more Merton Park productions and speaks fondly of his time there on his website saying it was 'an environment of incomparable studio friendliness and warmth.'

THE GRAND JUNCTION CASE (1961)

Directed by Peter Duffell

Screenplay by James Eastwood

Produced by Jack Greenwood

Starring: Russell Napier, Howard Pays, Wilfred Brambell, Kenneth J Warren

A fisherman pulls out a woman's leg, wrapped in sacking, from the Thames and reports it to police who then search for other body parts. After much searching they find an arm, also wrapped in sacking, which has on it a tattoo of an edelweiss. Due to the precision of the dismemberment they suspect it has been done by someone with some expertise.

The police team is led again by Inspector Duggan (Napier) and his sidekick Sergeant Adams (Pays). They find that the tattoo was not done in this country, but probably on the continent. Duggan then has to travel to Nice and interview a tattooist there.

The police pathologist in this episode is played by Wilfred Brambell.

Locations: no Merton Park shooting, but again atmosphere is added with other location shooting – e.g. the airport.

Notes: Wilfred Brambell had already been acting for over a decade, and the following year started his most famous role, as TV's Albert Steptoe. A couple of years after that he was starring in the Beatles' first film, A Hard Day's Night (1964).

THE NEVER NEVER MURDER (1961)

Directed by Peter Duffell

Screenplay by James Eastwood

Produced by Jack Greenwood

Starring: Russell Napier, Maurice Good, Genine Graham, Harriette Johns

Workmen discover the body of a woman behind a wall in the house they are demolishing. The police try to track down the previous occupants of the house and get on the trail of a man selling expensive household gadgets very cheaply. Is he somehow connected to the murder?

Once again, the hunt is led by Inspector Duggan (Napier) and this time his assistant is Sergeant Harper (Good).

It is noticeable that by this stage of the series there is more humour coming into it, albeit rather understated wry humour. Some of the characterisations too (in this episode by Fanny Carby and Brian Wilde) offer comedic contrast with the sometimes grisly murders.

Locations: A house in Sheridan Road, not far from the studios.

Notes: playing a small part is Brian Wilde, later famous as jail warder Mr Barrowclough in TV comedy series Porridge and Foggy in Last of the Summer Wine.

Also playing a small part was Fanny Carby who also appeared in some of the Edgar Wallace mysteries at Merton Park as well as in Sparrows Can't Sing (1963), also made at Merton Park.

WINGS OF DEATH (1961)

Directed by Allan Davis (Rheingold Theatre, Rogue's March, Love Among the Ruins)

Screenplay by James Eastwood

Produced by Jack Greenwood

Starring: Harry H Corbett, Simon Lack, Shelagh Fraser, Clinton Greyn

A light plane crashes, killing the pilot. At least, that's how it seems, but the pathology report reveals that he was dead before the crash. The police investigate, led by Superintendent Hammond (Corbett) and Sergeant Philips (Lack). The pilot's wife (Fraser) is a photographic model and the police question her at the studio where her male colleague interferes in the enquiry. Do they know something about the murder?

Locations: Nelson hospital, directly opposite the studios, is shown.

Notes: director Allan Davis worked with many big film stars both before and after this – e.g. Rheingold Theatre (1954) with Douglas Fairbanks Jr, Rogue's March (1953) with Peter Lawford and Love Among the Ruins (1975) with Laurence Olivier and Katherine Hepburn. The same year (1961) he also worked at Merton Park on the Edgar Wallace mystery The Fourth Square.

The following year (1962) Harry H Corbett was to begin his most famous role, that of Harold Steptoe in TV comedy series Steptoe and Son. His co-star, Wilfred Bramble, had just recently appeared in Scotland Yard episode The Grand Junction Case.

Peter Bowles played a small part as a policeman (his first film). Five years later he was in iconic sixties British film Blow Up (1966) then in the 1980s TV comedy series To The Manor Born.

THE SQUARE MILE MURDER (1961)

Directed by Allan Davis (Rogue's March, Clue of the Twisted Candle)

Screenplay by James Eastwood

Produced by Jack Greenwood

Starring: John Welsh, Stanley Morgan, Delphi Lawrence, Carl Jaffe

The manager of a travel agent's in the City of London opens his office door one morning to find the safe blown open and the safecracker himself lying dead on the floor. The man is known to the investigating policemen, Inspector Hicks (Welsh) and Sergeant Riley (Morgan).

The police question the safecracker's widow, but before long she too is killed.

The police find the gang behind the robbery and arrange for an ex-convict to get a job at the business premises of the ringleader to work undercover.

Locations: several local ones used including Wimbledon Broadway, the car showroom at Merton Rush (opposite the studios), Woolworth's in Morden, the Western bank at Wimbledon Chase, and Morden Road, South Wimbledon.

Notes: this was the last of the series before the similar Scales of Justice series started the following year, also produced by Jack Greenwood, with James Eastwood as writer and Edgar Lustgarten as host.

John Welsh also appeared in Konga, made at Merton Park that same year (1961). In 1957 he had appeared as a police inspector in Merton Park film The Counterfeit Plan.

Director Alan Davis's first film was Rogue's March (1953) starring 'Rat Pack' member Peter Lawford.

THE SCALES OF JUSTICE SERIES (1962–1967)

The Scotland Yard series finished in 1961 and the following year this series started, bearing some similarities. Again, the host was Edgar Lustgarten, but instead of introducing each episode from his book-lined study, he would introduce it from somewhere closer to the action, usually on the street.

The producer of the first episode, as on the Scotland Yard series, was Jack Greenwood and the screenwriter was James Eastwood, as it had been for many of the Scotland Yard episodes.

The main difference was that, as the title implies, the emphasis was on the judicial process of each crime, rather than simply the police work. However, this is not to say these were courtroom dramas. Most of each episode looks at the human story behind each crime and the police are rarely seen. The courtroom scene is usually simply the coda to the crime.

Each episode begins with pictures of the law courts in the Strand and of the Old Bailey. The 'Scales of Justice' refer to those in the left hand of Lady Justice, the statue that is on top of the Old Bailey. Unlike the American voice-over for the Scotland Yard series, the voice-over for Scales of Justice is very much RP English.

The theme tune played over the end credits is by The Tornados and was released as a single.

THE GUILTY PARTY (1962)

Directed by Lionel Harris (ITV Play of the Week 1956–63, BBC Wednesday Play 1966–68)

Screenplay by James Eastwood

Produced by Jack Greenwood

Starring: Zena Marshall, Jack Gwillim, Derek Francis, Anthony Jacobs

Edward Sinclair (Jacobs) is a seemingly rich man, with a younger, attractive wife (Marshall), and they are giving a party in their Mayfair home when a debt collector calls demanding money.

With only a day to pay Sinclair goes abroad, taking some of his wife's jewellery and suggests to her that she sees one of his male friends while he is away. When he comes back he accuses her of adultery.

Locations: no Merton Park locations.

Notes: that same year, Zena Marshall appeared in the very first Bond film, Dr No (1962). Also that year Jack Gwillim appeared in David Lean's Lawrence of Arabia (1962).

Director Lionel Harris was also an actor and had appeared in Powell and Pressburger's Tales of Hoffman (1951).

A WOMAN'S PRIVILEGE (1962)

Directed by Anthony Bushell (Long Dark Hall, The Terror of the Tongs)

Screenplay by James Eastwood

Produced by Jack Greenwood

Starring: Bernard Archard, Ann Lynn, Patrick Wymark

A man in his early 50s (Archard) meets a younger woman (Lynn) on a cruise ship and they plan to get married. However, when they get back to England and the man has sold his house and business in preparation for the marriage the woman changes her mind and he sues for breach of promise, a highly unusual course of action for a man.

Locations: St Mary's church, Merton Park and Wimbledon Village.

Notes: That same year Bernard Archard had appeared in another Merton Park production, Flat Two (1962), an Edgar Wallace mystery. He was later to appear in films such as Day of the Jackal (1973) and Roman Polanski's Macbeth (1971).

Patrick Wymark was late to appear in Repulsion (1965), Where Eagles Dare (1968) and Battle of Britain (1969).

Another actor in this film, Ernest Clark, had appeared in the Dam Busters (1955) and would later appear in Gandhi (1982) as well as many other high-profile films.

MOMENT OF DECISION (1962)

Directed by John Knight (Mail Van Murder, The Main Chance)

Screenplay by James Eastwood

Produced by Jack Greenwood

Starring: Ray Barrett, Patricia Healey, Viola Keats, Michael Sarne

A young German au pair girl has taken the baby in her charge to Wimbledon Common but when her boyfriend turns up they walk off and leave the baby unattended. When they come back the baby has been abducted by a woman who had recently lost her own baby. At first her husband is appalled, then realises that they can turn this to their advantage, especially when the baby's father offers a generous reward.

Locations: Wimbledon Common, Queen's Road and Haydon's Road, Wimbledon.

Notes: earlier that same year Mike Sarne had had a number one hit record with Come Outside (featuring Wendy Richards), and a follow-up top twenty hit with Will I What (featuring Billy Davis). He went on to many other acting and directing roles such as Myra Breckinridge

(1970) as director, and Tinker, Tailor, Soldier, Spy (2011) and Les Miserables (2012) as an actor.

Ray Barrett was a familiar face on British TV throughout the 1960s and 70s and beyond, appearing in series such as Emergency Ward 10, Z-Cars, Dixon of Dock Green etc. and the year before he died was in the film Australia (2008) with Nicole Kidman and Hugh Jackman.

POSITION OF TRUST (1963)

Directed by Lionel Harris (ITV Play of the Week 1956–63, BBC Wednesday Play 1966–68)

Screenplay by James Eastwood

Produced by Jack Greenwood

Starring: Derek Sherwin, Imogen Hassall, Edward Atienza, Peter Barkworth

A rebellious student (Sherwin) from a rich family gets kicked out of university and further disgraces himself by picking up a French student (Hassall) in a bar and taking her away for a weekend in Brighton where they are surprised by a private detective (Barkworth) entering their hotel bedroom, saying he has been employed by her husband.

The student attempts to pay off the detective, leading to further problems and, ultimately, a death. The episode has a nice, unexpected twist at the end.

Locations: no Merton Park locations.

Notes: Peter Barkworth went on to some high-profile film roles including Where Eagles Dare (1968) and Patton (1970).

Derek Sherwin was to appear again in the last episode of this series, Payment in Kind (1967).

THE UNDESIRABLE NEIGHBOUR (1963)

Directed by Gordon Hales (Return to Sender, editor on Village of the Damned)

Screenplay by James Eastwood

Produced by Jack Greenwood

Starring: Bridget Armstrong, Ronald Hatton, Vanda Godsell, Dorinda Stevens, Howard Pays

A young couple (Armstrong and Hatton) move into a new house on a modern estate and one of the women neighbours (Godsell) spies on the wife and accuses her of having affairs with various men. The wife eventually decides to take the neighbour to court for slander.

Locations: no Merton Park locations.

Notes: Garfield Morgan, who plays a barrister in the courtroom scene, later became best known for his role in TV's The Sweeney as Detective Chief Inspector Frank Haskins.

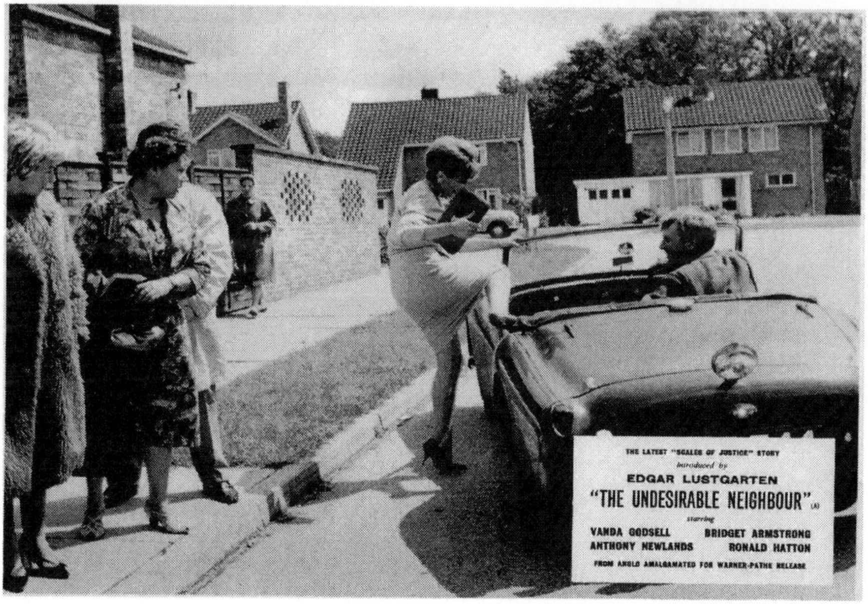

THE INVISIBLE ASSET (1963)

Directed by Norman Harrison (Locker 69, Incident at Midnight)

Screenplay by James Eastwood

Produced by Jack Greenwood

Starring: Kenneth J Warren, Ronald Leigh-Hunt, Annette Carell, Gabriella Licudi

It starts with restaurateur Sam Warren (Warren) in the bankruptcy court then goes into a flashback of his story. His restaurant was popular with city businessmen and, with hidden microphones, he got useful information that enabled him to make money but then lost it through gambling.

An acquaintance of his, Jimmy Donovan (Leigh Hunt) is blackmailing him about the hidden microphones so he and his wife decide to skip the country. But Donovan seems to be able to track their every move ...

Locations: no Merton Park locations.

Notes: Norman Harrison had directed at Merton Park the previous year – Edgar Wallace film Locker 69 (1962), and also that same year, another Edgar Wallace, Incident at Midnight (1963).

A couple of years later Kenneth J Warren was in the film High Wind in Jamaica (1965) with Anthony Quinn and James Coburn.

PERSONAL AND CONFIDENTIAL (1965)

Directed by Geoffrey Nethercott (Accidental Death, Who Was Maddox?)

Screenplay by James Eastwood

Produced by Jack Greenwood

Starring: Ellen McIntosh, Robert Cartland, Harry Littlewood, Howard Lang

A man is found dead on the ground outside the open window of his hotel room. In his briefcase are top secret government files. A woman he knew, Marion Corbett (McIntosh), who is PA to a government minister is questioned. The files found on the dead man had been in her keeping prior to his death and she pleads ignorance of how he came to have them.

Locations: no Merton Park locations.

Notes: Geoffrey Nethercott directed the Edgar Wallace mystery Accidental Death (1963) at Merton Park and was later a producer for films such as Blue Blood (1974) with Oliver Reed and Derek Jacobi and Merry Christmas Mr Lawrence (1983) with David Bowie and Tom Conti.

This was the first Scales of Justice episode since 1963; none were made in 1964.

THE HIDDEN FACE (1965)

Directed by Patrick Dromgoole (Design For Murder, Around the Corner – TV films)

Screenplay by James Eastwood

Produced by Jack Greenwood

Starring: Christine Finn, Richard Butler, Alex MacIntosh, Robert James

Social campaigner Ronald Milsom (William Sherwood) is strongly criticised in a book which brings his personal morals into doubt and he shoots himself dead. The writer of the book, Jane Penshurst (Finn) is taken to court and seems to have defended herself well when a surprise witness makes some startling revelations.

Locations: no Merton Park locations.

Notes: Derek Nimmo plays a small part as a barrister. A couple of years later he was to appear in the star-studded Casino Royale (1967) which was co-directed by Merton Park regular Ken Hughes and featured many actors who had appeared in Merton Park productions. Nimmo was to become best known for his role as Brother Dominic in TV comedy series Oh Brother!

MATERIAL WITNESS (1965)

Directed by Geoffrey Nethercott

Screenplay by James Eastwood

Produced by Jack Greenwood

Starring: Reginald Marsh, Noel Trevarthen, Sally Nesbitt, Sheila Manahan

Successful businessman Harry Turner is booked for drunk driving and serves a short jail sentence. While he's inside the young executive who hates him gets his job and starts seeing his daughter whom he eventually plans to marry. But things don't work out for the young couple quite as planned ...

Locations: no Merton Park locations.

Notes: Reginald Marsh had a long acting career, mainly in TV, but also played the Prince of Wales in Young Winston (1972) alongside Simon Ward, Robert Shaw and Anne Bancroft.

Noel Trevarthen later appeared in the Merton Park film It! (1967), starring Roddy McDowall and Jill Howarth.

COMPANY OF FOOLS (1966)

Directed by Peter Duffell

Screenplay by James Eastwood and Peter Duffell

Produced by Jack Greenwood

Starring: Barrie Ingham, Jacqueline Jones, Garfield Morgan, Maurice Kaufmann

The first of the series to be filmed in colour, and with its light-hearted, comedic aspect has a definite 'swinging sixties' feel to it, at times straying close to the style of one of the more whimsical episodes of The Avengers. Even Edgar Lustgarten allows himself a smile at the end.

It starts with angry shareholders reacting to the announcement of the collapse of a company they have invested in. Several of them get together afterwards to drown their sorrows and hatch a plan to take revenge on the company's owner, Jason (Morgan), whom they believe was complicit in allowing the company to fail.

The episode then goes into 'comedy caper' mode with one of the gang, Kasabis (Kaufmann) dressing up as an Arab and the other members of the group taking on various roles at a business meeting with Jason to trick him into doing an arms deal with the 'rich Arab'. The leader of the group is Major MacDonald (Ingham), a former military intelligence officer who has the expertise and authority to steer the plan.

It is a lot of fun and has an amusing sub-plot with the 'rich Arab' making a play for Jason's glamorous wife, Liz (Jones).

Locations: no Merton Park locations.

Notes: one of the gang is played by Frank Williams, later to become well-known for his role as the vicar in TV comedy series Dad's Army.

Many actors who appeared in Merton Park productions appeared in The Avengers. Maurice Kaufmann didn't, but in real life was married to Avengers star Honor Blackman.

That same year, Barrie Ingham had appeared in Merton Park sci-fi film, Invasion (1966), also as a major. He had also appeared in some of the Edgar Wallace mysteries at Merton Park. The previous year he had been in the film Doctor Who and the Daleks (1965) and was later to appear in Day of the Jackal (1973).

THE HAUNTED MAN (1966)

Directed by Stanley Willis

Screenplay by James Eastwood

Produced by Jack Greenwood

Starring: James Ellis, Keith Barron, Alexandra Bastedo, Isobel Black

An actor named Bill Kenton (Ellis) is suffering post-traumatic stress after trying to foil an armed robbery, has problems remembering lines and decides to take a break from acting. He is however, obsessed with trying to find the criminal he tried to tackle and believes he has found him in the person of Mark Godfrey (Barron) who is seemingly an honest and successful businessman. Kenton harasses him until he agrees to meet – with dire results.

Locations: The George inn, Morden and Crown House, Morden.

Notes: Stanley Willis had never directed before but had been editor on Merton Park's Limping Man (1953) starring Lloyd Bridges.

James Ellis had been in TV series Z-Cars since 1962 as PC Lynch and was to continue in the role (with a couple of promotions!) until 1978

INFAMOUS CONDUCT (1966)

Directed by Richard Martin (Compact, Dr Who – TV series)

Screenplay by James Eastwood

Produced by Jack Greenwood

Starring: Dermot Walsh, Bridget Armstrong, Richard Warner, Ewan Solon

Surgeon Anthony Searle is struck off for alleged sexual misconduct with a patient and meets a young woman artist (Armstrong) with whom he has an affair. She, however, involves him in carrying out surgery on members of the underworld whom she knows.

Locations: no Merton Park locations.

Notes: Dermot Walsh had appeared in Merton Park films Ghost Ship (1952) with Hazel Court, The Floating Dutchman (also 1952) with Sydney Tafler and Undercover Agent (1953) also with Hazel Court.

Bridget Armstrong had already appeared in a previous Scales of Justice episode, the Undesirable Neighbour (1963).

PAYMENT IN KIND (1967)

Directed by Peter Duffell

Screenplay by John Roddick

Produced by Jack Greenwood

Starring: Justine Lord, Maxine Audley, Brian Haines, Derek Sherwin

Young mother Paula (Lord) is visited by Andrews (Sherwin) who collects HP payments that she is struggling to pay. He offers to help her out but she refuses, sensing that he may have other intentions. When she does eventually manage to pay him off he gives her a lift in his car, then drives to a deserted farm and sexually assaults her. She fights back with tragic results.

This episode is more graphic than earlier episodes and has one genuinely shocking moment. There are even shades of Hitchcock in it.

Locations: Wimbledon Common (near the windmill).

Notes: Maxine Audley had appeared in Michael Powell's controversial Peeping Tom (1960).

Brian Haines had been in Merton Park film It! (1967) starring Roddy McDowall and Jill Howarth.

Derek Sherwin had been in the earlier Scales of Justice episode, Position of Trust (1963).

Although James Eastwood had written every other episode of this series, this final one was by John Roddick who had written several of the screenplays for Merton Park's Edgar Wallace series as well as episodes of The Saint and Danger Man.

EDGAR WALLACE MYSTERIES (1960–1965)

Loosely based on the stories of Edgar Wallace these one-hour films did not stick to the era in which they were originally set but were updated to contemporary settings and sometimes even the titles were changed too.

They were originally intended as supporting cinema features but have been widely shown on TV in the years since.

Each episode began with a mist-enshrouded bust of Wallace rotating as the titles and title music played. The theme tune, Man of Mystery, was later recorded by The Shadows and became a hit.

URGE TO KILL (1960)

Directed by Vernon Sewell

Screenplay by James Eastwood (based on the novel by Gerald Savory)

Produced by Jack Greenwood

Starring: Patrick Barr, Howard Pays, Ruth Dunning, Terence Knapp

A young woman is murdered at the beginning and suspicion falls on the simple-minded Hughie (Knapp) who has an odd obsession with collecting jagged pieces of glass and pottery (the woman had been slashed with something sharp).

Hughie lives with his aunt (Dunning) who cannot believe the young man is capable of such a crime, though some of the villagers who gather at the local pub think otherwise.

The aunt takes in lodgers, played by Howard Pays and Wilfred Brambell, who also come under suspicion. Then, a second young woman is murdered ...

It's an atmospheric piece with a 'kitchen-sink' drama feel to it and doesn't seem constrained by its budgetary limitations. Some good performances, particularly from Knapp, who, despite his simple innocence, could, just could, be the murderer.

This is sometimes regarded as the first of the series but was not based on an Edgar Wallace story. It does however, have the usual 'revolving bust' title sequence and theme tune.

Locations: no Merton Park locations.

Notes: the original novel on which this was based was Hughie Roddis by Gerald Savory, published in 1942. In 1944 there was a stage version by Savory and Charles K Freeman.

Just two years after this Wilfred Brambell was to make his first appearance as Albert Steptoe in long-running TV comedy series Steptoe and Son.

CLUE OF THE TWISTED CANDLE (1960)

Directed by Alan Davis (Rheingold Theatre, Rogue's March, Love Among the Ruins)

Screenplay by Philip Mackie

Produced by Jack Greenwood

Starring: Bernard Lee, Anthony Baird, Francis De Wolff

A man named Karadis (de Wolff) asks the police to have a direct telephone line installed so that he can contact them immediately if his life is threatened. They suspect that he may not be an entirely honest character but agree.

Meanwhile, a friend of Karadis, named Lexman has received a blackmail note which Karadis burns. He also gives him a gun for protection. Another friend of Karadis, named Viney, goes to Lexman's house and as his driver waits outside a shot is heard. Viney is found dead and when the police arrive Lexman tells them it was an accident. He explains that he was being blackmailed but when Karadis is questioned he denies all knowledge of the blackmail letter.

The police, led by Superintendent Meredith (Lee), intend to get to the bottom of it and find out what exactly Karadis is up to.

Locations: no Merton Park locations.

Notes: just a couple of years later, Bernard Lee was to make his first appearance as M in the Bond films with Dr No (1962). He still found time though to reprise his role as Superintendent Meredith in three more Edgar Wallace mysteries between 1961 and 1964, culminating in Who Killed Maddox (1964). He was also in the 1961 episode, Partners in Crime, but this time as Inspector Mann.

Francis De Wolff also appeared in Bond film From Russia With Love (1963) and another Merton Park film, Devil Doll (1964).

MARRIAGE OF CONVENIENCE (1960)

Directed by Clive Donner (What's New Pussycat, Here We Go Round the Mulberry Bush)

Screenplay by Robert Banks Stewart

Produced by Jack Greenwood

Starring: Harry H Corbett, John Cairney, Jennifer Daniel, John Van Eyssen

A prisoner named Larry Wilson (Cairney) is temporarily released to get married at a registry office but manages to escape.

He tries to find the girlfriend he left on the outside, who just happens to have the entire proceeds of the crime he is serving time for, but she has disappeared – with the policeman who arrested him!

A good cast, with Harry H Corbett adding some humour to his role as investigating officer Inspector Bruce, and some fun minor characters who add to the enjoyment.

Locations: Watery Lane and Manor Gardens, opposite the studio, and Kingston town hall.

Notes: Clive Donner was soon to go on to much bigger things, directing Alan Bates in The Guest (based on Pinter's The Caretaker, 1963), Peter Sellers in Woody Allen's What's New Pussycat (1965) and Peter O'Toole in Rogue Male (1976).

Screenwriter Robert Banks Stewart was also to go on to write for many TV series including The Human Jungle, Danger Man, The Avengers, Callan, The Sweeney, and many more and also created the series Shoestring starring Trevor Eve. This Edgar Wallace mystery was his first screenplay.

THE MAN WHO WAS NOBODY (1960)

Directed by Montgomery Tully (Third Alibi, Boy With a Flute, Query)

Screenplay by James Eastwood

Produced by Jack Greenwood

Starring: Hazel Court, Lisa Daniely, John Crawford, Paul Eddington

A man named Tynewood spends £8000 on a ring for his girlfriend but the jeweller later finds that the cheque has bounced. Tynewood disappears but his lawyer hires private detective Marjorie Stedman (Court) to track him down and also to warn him that' South Africa Smith' is back in town.

Stedman then enters an underworld of beatniks, private gambling dens and shifty characters in her quest. Then Tynewood's body is found in the Thames, not drowned, but strangled.

Locations: no Merton Park locations.

Notes: John Crawford went on to some big films, including The Poseidon Adventure (1972) and The Towering Inferno (1974).

Paul Eddington became a household name in the 1970s through comedy series The Good Life and Yes, Minister, though he had appeared in many popular TV series in the 1960s such as The Avengers and The Prisoner.

It is interesting to see a woman detective in a film of this vintage – thirty years before Helen Mirren played a Metropolitan police detective in TV's Prime Suspect.

PARTNERS IN CRIME (1961)

Directed by Peter Duffell (The Avengers, Man in a Suitcase)

Screenplay by Robert Banks Stewart

Produced by Jack Greenwood

Starring: Bernard Lee, Moira Redmond, John Van Eyssen, Stanley Morgan

Businessman Harold Strickland (Victor Platt) returns home with his wife to find his safe has been broken open, he then sees a figure in the doorway who shoots him dead. His wife seems distraught, but when her husband's business partner Merril (Van Eyssen) visits the next day they kiss passionately.

Inspector Mann (Lee) investigates and initially works on the assumption that it is a robbery that has gone wrong, until, by a lucky chance, the gun turns up.

A good episode, and Lee is excellent as the inspector with his world-weary demeanour and gallows humour.

This episode also has, for a low-budget film, quite a spectacular ending.

Locations: Kenley Road and Keswick Avenue in Merton Park, plus some nearby streets in Earslfield are used.

Notes: in his other appearances as a police inspector in the series Bernard Lee is known as Meredith, but this time he is Mann. Similarly, Stanley Morgan's police sergeant is usually Anson, but this time he is Rutledge.

THE CLUE OF THE NEW PIN (1961)

Directed by Alan Davis

Screenplay by Philip Mackie

Produced by Jack Greenwood

Starring: Paul Daneman, James Villiers, Katherinee Woodville, Clive Morton

Rich and irascible John Tredmere (David Horne) is being pestered by TV presenter Tab Holland (Villiers) for an interview but promises he will tell him nothing. He does however show him his underground vault in which he keeps all his treasures and to which there is only one key.

We later find that Tredmere has been murdered and his body is inside the locked vault – with the solitary key inside too, on a table.

Tab, and the investigating police officer, Superintendent Carver (Bernard Archard) are baffled as to how the key ended up inside the locked vault.

The police inspector suspects that Tredmere's nephew, Rex Lander (Daneman) might be involved but cannot fully explain it.

Notes: Paul Daneman also appeared in two other Edgar Wallace episodes, Fourth Square (1961) and Locker 69 (1962) and later appeared in Zulu (1964) which also starred Merton Park actors Stanley Baker, Michael Caine and James Booth (and one or two others), and How I Won the War (1967) with Merton Park actors Michael Crawford and Lee Montague (and others).

THE FOURTH SQUARE (1961)

Directed by Allan Davis

Screenplay by James Eastwood

Produced by Jack Greenwood

Starring: Conrad Phillips, Natashas Parry, Delphi Lawrence, Paul Daneman

A domestic safe is broken into and a piece of emerald jewellery is stolen. The thief leaves behind two squares of paper stuck to the wall before murdering the maid who tries to follow him. Similar squares have been left at a previous robbery. The woman who owns the jewellery, Nina Stewart (Lawrence), tells the police nothing has been stolen, but asks her lawyer to investigate privately.

Locations: no Merton Park locations.

Notes: something of a star-studded cast. Conrad Phillips had appeared the previous year in Sons & Lovers (1960) with Trevor Howard, Natasha Parry had appeared the previous year in Midnight Lace (1960) with Doris Day and Rex Harrison and Delphi Lawrence was to appear in Bunny Lake is Missing (1965) with Laurence Olivier. Miriam Karlin, who has a small role in this, also that year started her most famous role as militant trade union rep Paddy Fleming in TV comedy series The Rag Trade.

THE MAN AT THE CARLTON TOWER (1961)

Directed by Robert Tronson (Number Six, Ring of Treason, Act of Reprisal)

Screenplay by Philip Mackie

Produced by Jack Greenwood

Starring: Maxine Audley, Lee Montague, Allan Cuthbertson, Alfred Burke, Terence Alexander

A thief robs a jeweller's shop but when a passing policeman tries to prevent him escaping he is shot dead. Meanwhile a character by the name of Harry Stone (Burke) is booking a room in a hotel and is recognised by an ex-policeman, but claims to be someone else. We next see him attempting to become a member of a private club and being refused, but claiming to know the owner.

Locations: no Merton Park locations, but the real Carlton Tower hotel in Knightsbridge was used for some of the filming. It had just opened in 1961

Notes: another episode with high-profile actors. Maxine Audley had appeared the previous year in Michael Powell's Peeping Tom (1960), Lee Montague had appeared in Moulin Rouge (1952) with Zsa Zsa Gabor and was to appear in How I Won The War (1967) with Michael Crawford and John Lennon. By coincidence, there is a policeman in this episode by the name of Sergeant Pepper, which was the title of the album that the Beatles released in 1967, the year Montague appeared in How I Won The War with Lennon.

Alfred Burke was later to become well-known as TV detective Frank Marker in Public Eye, and Terence Alexander was Hungerford in long-running detective series Bergerac (the producer of which, for several episodes, was Robert Tronson, director of this Edgar Wallace episode). Nyree Dawn Porter, whose film career had only begun the previous year, also appeared in this and just six years later was to star in prestigious TV series The Forsyte Saga as Irene Forsyte.

THE CLUE OF THE SILVER KEY (1961)

Directed by Gerard Glaister (The Partner, The Set Up, The Share Out)

Screenplay by Philip Mackie

Produced by Jack Greenwood

Starring: Bernard Lee, Stanley Morgan, Patrick Cargill, Finlay Currie

Harvey Lane (Currie) is a cantankerous, rich old man, waited on by a faithful butler (Cargill). He has refused to allow his niece Mary (Jennifer Daniel) to marry and so we know that her boyfriend Gerry (Lyndon Brook) has a grudge against him. When Lane is later found shot dead suspicion falls upon Gerry but is it that straightforward?

Inspector Meredith (Lee) also has two other murders to solve – are they connected?

Bernard Lee and Stanley Morgan reprise their roles from earlier episode The Clue of the Twisted Candle as Inspector Meredith and Sergeant Anson and begin to develop the sort of banter and joshing that we associate with later police double acts such as Carter and Regan from The Sweeney. Despite thc three murders there is quite a bit of comedy in the episode, often involving the hapless and hopeless rookie copper PC Quigley (Derek Sherwin).

Locations: no Merton Park locations.

Notes: A lot of well-known faces in this episode including Sam Kydd, Anthony Sharp, who went on to appear in A Clockwork Orange (1971), Barry Lyndon (1975) and Never Say Never Again (1983), and Patrick Cargill who appeared in A Stitch in Time (1963) and Help! (1965) as well as various Carry On films and numerous TV comedy series.

ATTEMPT TO KILL (1961)

Directed by Royston Morley (Armchair Mystery Theatre – TV)

Screenplay by Richard Harris

Produced by Jack Greenwood

Starring: Tony Wright, Richard Pearson, Freda Jackson

Self-made millionaire Frank Weyman fires one of his employees, Fraser (Denis Holmes) whom he thinks is interested in his fiancée.

Weyman then experiences 'accidents' that appear to be attempts by someone to injure, or even kill him. The police are called in to investigate, but then there is a surprise death ...

Locations: no Merton Park locations.

Notes: Richard Pearson is another example of an actor that had a high-profile career both before and after his work at Merton Park. He had appeared in A Christmas Carol (1951) with Alastair Sim and then in Sunday Bloody Sunday (1971) with Peter Finch and Glenda Jackson and The Mirror Crack'd (1980) with Tony Curtis and Angela Lansbury.

Screenwriter Richard Harris went on to write for many TV series including Hancock, The Avengers, Darling Buds of May and A Touch of Frost.

MAN DETAINED (1961)

Directed by Robert Tronson

Screenplay by Richard Harris

Produced by Jack Greenwood

Starring: Bernard Archard, Elvi Hale, Paul Stassino, Michael Coles

Secretary Kay Simpson (Hale) discovers her boss's safe has been broken into but he is angry when she tells him she has informed the police. The thief has got away with £10,000 but the boss doesn't tell police about this, only that £20 petty cash has been stolen.

Police inspector Verity (Archard) investigates but finds more questions than answers. Then the boss, Thomas Maple (Victor Platt), is found dead. They pick up the thief, Frank Murray (Coles), who admits the robbery but denies killing Maple.

A very good episode, with lots of action and suspense, putting one in mind of a more modern police show such as The Sweeney, using as it does, atmospheric locations, car chases, etc.

Locations: no Merton Park locations, but other South London ones used, including railway sidings, warehouses and other downbeat backdrops.

Notes: Bernard Archard played a police inspector in earlier episode, The Clue of the New Pin, but was given the name of Superintendent Carver.

Four years after appearing in this Paul Stassino got not one, but two parts in the Bond film Thunderball (1965).

NEVER BACK LOSERS (1961)

Directed by Robert Tronson

Screenplay by Lukas Heller

Produced by Jack Greenwood

Starring: Jack Hedley, Jacqueline Ellis, Patrick Magee, Richard Warner

Another good episode with lots of atmosphere – the race track, dodgy drinking clubs, poker games, gun-toting girls, etc.

Jockey Wally Sanders (George Tovey) loses a race he was expected to win. Next thing he is coshed over the head after leaving a pub and his car is then found crashed with him badly injured at the wheel.

An insurance investigator named Jim Mathews (Hedley) looks into the accident claim but finds himself in a unsavoury underworld where he too gets beaten up and told to mind his own business.

Patrick Magee is on form as sinister gangland boss Ben Black and the episode moves on at a brisk pace.

Locations: quite a lot of filming in and around Merton Park: Martin Way, Martin Grove, Kenley Road, and the Leather Bottle pub (right next door to the studios).

Notes: writer Lukas Heller had a high profile screenwriting career. The year after this he wrote the screenplay for Whatever Happened to Baby Jane (1962) starring Bette Davis and Joan Crawford; he also co-wrote the screenplays for The Flight of the Phoenix (1965) starring Richard Attenborough and James Stewart and for The Dirty Dozen (1967) starring Lee Marvin and Charles Bronson – as well as many other screenplays. This was his first film script.

This episode is full of well-known faces, including Larry Taylor who had appeared in Alexander the Great (1956) with Richard Burton, and several actors who would be remembered from Ealing comedies etc.

THE SINISTER MAN (1961)

Directed by Clive Donner (What's New Pussycat, Here We Go Round the Mulberry Bush)

Screenplay by Robert Banks Stewart

Produced by Jack Greenwood

Starring: John Bentley, Patrick Allen, Jacqueline Ellis

A lock keeper finds a dead body in the Thames and reports it to the police. The body turns out to be that of a professor of Oriental Studies at Oxford who had been working on some priceless artefacts from the fictional country of Kytang. He appears to have been killed by a karate chop. The artefacts have disappeared and the police, led by Superintendent Wills (Bentley) start to question the professor's erstwhile colleagues at Oxford.

Locations: no Merton Park locations, but quite a lot of other real locations (rather than stock footage) used, such as the River Thames, Oxford University, etc.

Notes: the lock keeper was played by Wilfred Brambell. Bert Kwouk, who has a small part near the end of the film, was to become best-known for his role as Cato in the Pink Panther films.

BACKFIRE (1961)

Directed by Paul Almond (Final Assignment, Ups and Downs)

Screenplay by Robert Banks Stewart

Produced by Jack Greenwood

Starring: Alfred Burke, Zena Marshall, Oliver Johnston, Noel Trevarthen

Cosmetics firm Venetia is in financial trouble with piles of unsold stock so the boss's right-hand man, Mitchell Logan (Burke), suggests an 'accidental' fire so they can claim on the insurance. The elderly boss, Bernard Curzon (Johnston), reluctantly agrees but the fire has several unanticipated consequences, including a death.

A good episode with plenty of pace and a plausible villain in Alfred Burke.

Locations: no Merton Park locations.

Notes: Zena Marshall, who plays Mrs Logan, was to appear the following year in Dr No (1962). Suzanne Neve, who played Curzon's daughter was to appear in TV series The Forsyte Saga from 1967, and was also in Scrooge (1970) with Albert Finney.

CANDIDATE FOR MURDER (1962)

Directed by David Villiers (Four Winds Island)

Screenplay by Lukas Heller

Produced by Jack Greenwood

Starring: Michael Gough, Hans Von Borsody, Erika Remberg, Vanda Godsell

Businessman Donald Edwards (Gough), hires German hitman Kersten (Von Borsody), to kill his wife actress Helene (Remberg) whom he suspects is having an affair. When it comes to payment however, Edwards wants proof that his wife is dead and Kersten isn't keen to provide it.

Helene's boyfriend, Robert Vaughan (John Justin) becomes involved when Helene does not board a plane that was due to take her abroad on an acting job.

A fast-moving episode with plenty of action and location shooting with one or two surprises along the way. Michael Gough plays his part with cultured menace and helps to make this one of the better Edgar Wallace films.

Locations: no Merton Park locations, but quite a bit of outside filming along country roads, deserted buildings, waste land, etc.

Notes: Hans Von Borsody was Austrian and appeared in many German language films but was also in A Bridge Too Far (1977) with Sean Connery, Michael Caine and Ryan O'Neal.

Michael Gough appeared in many films made at Merton Park, including Horrors of the Black Museum (1959), Konga (1961) and The Corpse (1971) as well as another Edgar Wallace episode, Game For Three Losers (1965).

Erika Remberg starred in cult classic Circus of Horrors (1960).

David Villiers had only directed one feature film prior to this, Four Winds Island, a CFF (Children's Film Foundation) film made at Merton Park in 1961. He also wrote the screenplay for another CFF film, Night Cargoes (1962) which starred a young Steve Marriott, later to become lead singer of the Small Faces.

FLAT TWO (1962)

Directed by Alan Cooke (Armchair Theatre, Wednesday Play – TV)

Screenplay by Lindsay Galloway

Produced by Jack Greenwood

Starring: John Le Mesurier, Bernard Archard, Jack Watling, Ann Bell

A young woman named Susan (Bell) has managed to rack up a £10,000 debt to casino owner Louba (David Bauer), who offers to write it off if she takes a holiday with him. Susan's boyfriend, Frank (Watling) threatens to kill him.

Later, Louba receives a letter containing a threat to kill him which he shows to the police.

Meanwhile, an old business associate of Louba's, Charles Berry (Barry Keegan) turns up with a score to settle. Louba, of course, ends up dead, but who did it? Inspector Trainer (Archard) investigates.

Locations: no Merton Park locations.

Notes: apart from his well-known role as Sergeant Wilson in TV comedy series Dads Army, John Le Mesurier had a long acting career going back to the 1930s and had appeared in such high-profile films as I'm All Right Jack (1959) with Peter Sellers and Richard Attenborough (both of whom had made films at Merton Park) and School for Scoundrels (1960) with Terry-Thomas and Ian Carmichael (both of whom also had made films at Merton Park).

THE SHARE OUT (1962)

Directed by Gerard Glaister (Clue of the Silver Key, The Set Up)

Screenplay by Philip Mackie

Produced by Jack Greenwood

Starring: Bernard Lee, Alexander Knox, Moira Redmond, William Russell

A gang of corporate crooks uses blackmail to persuade people to sell their properties at well below the market rate. They are led by Colonel Calderwood (Knox) and none of them trusts any of the others – with good reason.

Superintendent Meredith (Lee) becomes aware of the racket and decides he needs someone to infiltrate the gang and report back to him. He uses private detective Mike Stafford (Russell) who complicates things by immediately beginning an affair with one of the gang, Diana Marsh (Redmond).

Lots of intrigue, double-crossing, red herrings and one or two murders. Excellent cast headed by the ever-reliable Bernard Lee who plays the seasoned copper to perfection.

Locations: no Merton Park locations.

Notes: surprising to see an actor with Alexander Knox's pedigree in this. He had been in films since the early 1930s, appearing in The Sea Wolf (1941) with Edward G Robinson and playing the lead role of Woodrow Wilson in Darryl F Zanuck's Wilson (1944). Also, in the same year that he appeared in this he was in The Longest Day with John Wayne and Richard Burton.

NUMBER SIX (1962)

Directed by Robert Tronson

Screenplay by Philip Mackie

Produced by Jack Greenwood

Starring: Ivan Desny, Nadia Regin, Michael Goodliffe, Brian Bedford

Charles Valentine (Desny) is suspected of being involved in the killing of five women over the past decade but police have been unable to prove anything. He is now in London doing business and Detective Superintendent Hallett (Goodliffe) has him tailed by a mysterious character known only as Number Six.

Meanwhile, a man named Jimmy Gale (Bedford) saves Valentine from being stabbed by a waiter, killing him in the process and disposing of the body. He now feels Valentine owes him something. Jimmy has a rich, female friend named Nadia (Regin) who has an affair with Valentine. Is he going to be Valentine's next victim? Then there is the manservant that Valentine hires, but who seems to have a grudge against him.

Locations: no Merton Park locations.

Notes: Ivan Desny had appeared in Anastasia (1956) with Yul Brynner and Ingrid Bergmann. Nadia Rejin was to appear the year after this in Bond film From Russia With Love (1963) and the year after that in Goldfinger (1964), though still came back for another Merton Park Edgar Wallace film, Downfall (1964), and had also appeared in a second 1962 Merton Park Wallace film, Solo For Sparrow.

TIME TO REMEMBER (1962)

Directed by Charles Jarrott (Anne of the Thousand Days, Mary, Queen of Scots, Lost Horizon)

Screenplay by Arthur La Bern

Produced by Jack Greenwood

Starring: Harry H Corbett, Ray Barrett, Yvonne Monlaur, David Lodge

When the police arrive at the scene of a house robbery one of the criminals climbs onto the roof, pursued by a policeman and falls to the ground. He has though had time to drop the stolen jewellery down a chimney.

The crook, Jumbo Johnson (Lodge) is visited in hospital by his wife and just before he dies tells her about the jewellery. She then attempts to buy the house through estate agent Jack Burgess (Corbett) who manages to guess the reason and decides to buy the house himself. However, when he attempts to retrieve the jewellery he is disturbed by one of the gang.

Locations: no Merton Park locations.

Notes: This was the first film that Charles Jarrott directed and he went on to much bigger things, directing Anne of the Thousand Days (1969) starring Richard Burton, Mary, Queen of Scots (1971) starring Glenda Jackson and Vanessa Redgrave, and Lost Horizon (1973) starring Peter Finch and Liv Ullman.

Writer Arthur La Bern went on to write the novel Goodbye Piccadilly, Farewell Leicester Square (1966) on which Alfred Hitchcock's film Frenzy was based. He had also written the novel It Always Rains on Sunday on which the 1947 film of the same name was based, starring Googie Withers and Jack Warner.

SOLO FOR SPARROW (1962)

Directed by Gordon Flemyn (Dr Who & the Daleks, The Army Game, Philby, Burgess & Maclean)

Screenplay by Roger Marshall (based on the novel by Edgar Wallace)

Produced by Jack Greenwood

Starring: Glyn Houston, Anthony Newlands, Yvonne Buckingham

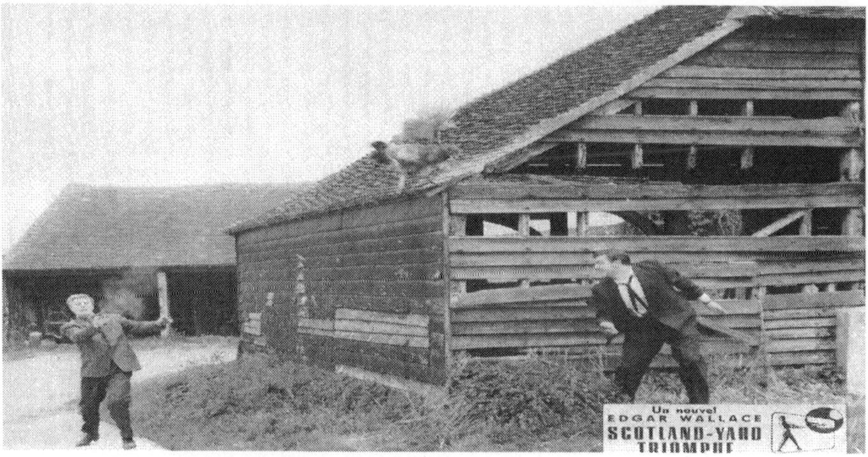

Notable for having Michael Caine in a small part (he is shown above). He plays Paddy Mooney, a member of a gang that kidnaps a woman as part of a robbery.

Glyn Houston plays Inspector Sparrow, who is taken off the case in favour of Scotland Yard detectives, but decides to take some leave and make his own investigations which complicate things somewhat. His maverick tendencies and attitude are almost like a forerunner to John Thaw's Jack Regan character in the Sweeney.

A good film with plot twists, action and effective character acting.

Locations: Several locations near Merton Park studios are used: Wimbledon Common, Wimbledon Village, Kingston Road, Mostyn Road and Watery Lane (directly opposite the studios), and the Leather Bottle pub which was the local for many people working at the studios over the years, being as it was literally next door.

Notes: The following year Yvonne Buckingham played the title role in The Christine Keeler Story (1963). Murray Melvin has a small, but scene-stealing part as a criminal electronics wizard. The following year he was to have a slightly larger role in the Merton Park film Sparrows Can't Sing with Barbara Windsor and James Booth. In 1966 he was to appear in Alfie with Michael Caine and another Merton Park regular, Sydney Tafler.

PLAYBACK (1962)

Directed by Quentin Lawrence (Cash on Demand, Secret of Blood Island)

Screenplay by Robert Banks Stewart

Produced by Jack Greenwood

Starring: Barry Foster, Margit Saad, Dinsdale Landen, Victor Platt

Young policeman Dave Hollis (Foster) gets involved with an attractive married woman named Lisa Shillack (Saad) and begins to accumulate debts at a gambling club which he is struggling to pay. Shillack then suggests that Dave should kill her husband.

A very good episode with very natural characters and a plot that builds throughout to a dramatic finale.

Locations: no Merton Park locations; in fact very little outside shooting.

Notes: The previous year Margit Saad had appeared in The Rebel (1961) with Tony Hancock and the year before that in another Merton Park film, The Criminal (1960) with Stanley Baker.

Barry Foster was to appear in many high-profile films, including The Family Way (1966) with Hayley Mills, Ryan's Daughter (1970) with Robert Mitchum and Trevor Howard, and Hitchcock's Frenzy (1972).

LOCKER 69 (1962)

Directed by Norman Harrison (Calculated Risk, The Crawling Eye)

Screenplay by Richard Harris

Produced by Jack Greenwood

Starring: Edward Underdown, Eddie Byrne, Paul Daneman, Clarissa Stolz

Businessman Bennet Sanders Underdown) has been doing some shady deals but his partner, John Griffiths (Daneman) has been keeping records in a safe deposit box and threatens to expose him if he continues.

Sanders' private detective then finds him murdered at home and when he takes a closer look is himself hit over the head. When he comes to and is questioned by police Sanders' body and the murder weapon, a knife, are nowhere to be seen.

It is quite a complicated plot with lots of characters, including an American journalist, Simon York (Byrne) who for some reason is allowed to accompany the police as they investigate.

There is a surprise plot twist later in the story when all is revealed.

Locations: no Merton Park locations.

Notes: Eddie Byrne had a long career in films, appearing in the Gentle Gunman (1952) with Dirk Bogarde and John Mills and also the first Star Wars film in 1977.

Edward Underdown later appeared in Doctor Terror's House of Horrors (1961) with Christopher Lee and Peter Cushing as well as Thunderball (1965). He had also been in another Merton Park film, The Dark Man (1951) with William Hartnell and Maxwell Reed.

DEATH TRAP (1962)

Directed by John Llewellyn Moxey (The City of the Dead, Foxhole in Cairo)

Screenplay by John Roddick

Produced by Jack Greenwood

Starring: Albert Leiven, Mercy Haystead, Kenneth Cope, Barbara Shelley

Company boss Paul Heindrich (Leiven) has a visit from a woman who is the sister of one of his ex-clients, who drew out her entire life savings before committing suicide. Was he somehow involved?

Inspector Simons (Leslie Sands) investigates, and Heindrich's secretary, Jean Anscomb (Shelley) also becomes suspicious and gets involved, incurring the displeasure of Heindrich.

Kenneth Cope plays Heindrich's stepson who also gets on the wrong side of him.

Some light relief is provided by a tramp (Richard Bird) who finds a dumped car that killed someone and has links to Heindrich.

Locations: no Merton Park locations.

Notes: The previous year Albert Leiven had appeared in Guns of Navarone (1961) with Gregory Peck and David Niven.

Barbara Windsor plays a small part as a girl in a shower. The following year she starred in the Merton Park film Sparrows Can't Sing (1963) directed by Joan Littlewood. She later appeared of course in many of the Carry On films, as did Kenneth Cope.

THE SET UP (1963)

Directed by Gerard Glaister

Screenplay by Roger Marshall

Produced by Jack Greenwood

Starring: Maurice Denham, Anthony Bate, Brian Peck, Luanshya Greer

Just released from prison, Arthur Payne (Peck) is travelling on a train without a valid ticket and is unable to pay the inspector. Fellow passenger Theo Gaunt (Denham) offers to pay and also says he might be able to give him a job. Later, a colleague of Gaunt's, Ray Underwood (Bate) visits Payne and offers him money to stage a robbery from a safe which is later shown to contain a gun as well as valuables. Payne is disturbed by a woman whom he shoots.

Payne goes on the run, pursued by Inspector Jackson (John Carson). But why has Payne been set up in this way?

Locations: no Merton Park locations.

Notes: That same year Maurice Denham also appeared in The Very Edge (1963) with Richard Todd and Anne Heywood and Paranoiac (1963) with Oliver Reed and Janette Scott.

The previous year John Carson had appeared in Guns of Darkness (1962) with Leslie Caron and David Niven.

INCIDENT AT MIDNIGHT (1963)

Directed by Norman Harrison (Locker 69)

Screenplay by Arthur La Bern

Produced by Jack Greenwood

Starring: Anton Diffring, Justine Lord, William Sylvester

An unusual setting – an all-night chemists, where a Doctor Schroeder, who has been struck off, regularly attends to collect his prescription. While there one night he recognises a former Nazi war criminal, Doctor Leichner (Diffring) who tells him he is not who he thinks he is. Leichner is running a drugs racket and is set to make a million.

Then a couple of crooks armed with a gun bring an injured colleague in and demand medical treatment for him. Dr Schroeder reluctantly agrees to help.

Quite a confusing plot, though entertaining in places, but has perhaps too much dialogue.

Locations: no Merton Park locations.

Notes: several well-known faces in the supporting cast including Warren Mitchell, later famous in TV comedy series Till Death Us Do Part as Alf Garnett, and Geoffrey Palmer, who appeared in many TV comedy series, including Butterflies, As Times Goes By and The Fall and Rise of Reginald Perrin.

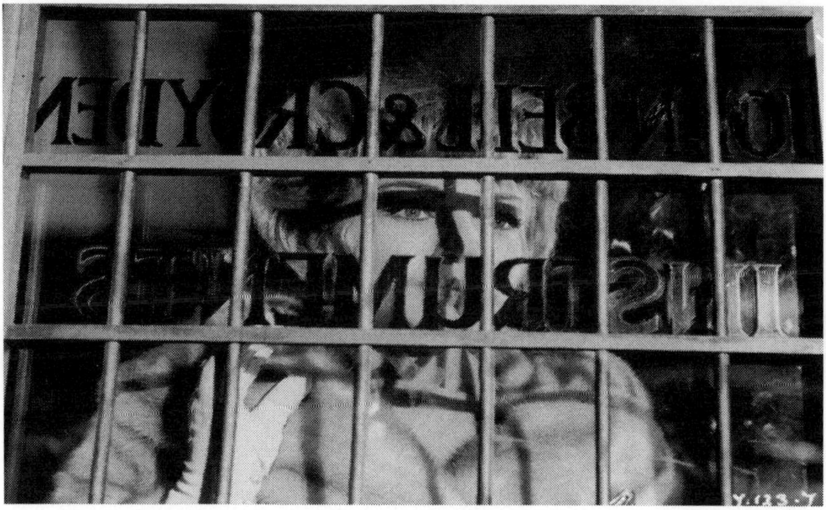

Incident at Midnight

THE £20,000 KISS (1963)

Directed by John Llewellyn Moxey (The City of the Dead, Foxhole in Cairo)

Screenplay by Philip Mackie

Produced by Jack Greenwood

Starring: Michael Goodliffe, Dawn Addams, Anthony Newlands, Alfred Burke

Politician Sir Harold Trevitt (Goodliffe) is called upon by neighbour Maxine Hagen (Addams) as she thinks there is an intruder and her husband is away. He reassures her and they kiss, but are seen by the maid, Paula, who blackmails them. Sir Harold employs a private detective to see if the maid has a history of blackmailing people, and he in turn involves Scotland Yard detective Inspector Waveney (Burke).

A good episode with lots of twists and turns along the way and a good supporting cast including Paul Whitsun Jones as the scurrilous gossip columnist Charles Pinder.

Locations: no Merton Park locations.

Notes: a couple of years later Michael Goodliffe was to appear in Von Ryan's Express (1965) with Frank Sinatra and Trevor Howard. Both Anthony Newlands and Alfred Burke appeared in several of the Edgar Wallace episodes made at Merton Park and the latter also starred in the successful detective series Public Eye (1965–75).

ON THE RUN (1963)

Directed by Robert Tronson (Never Back Losers, Man Detained)

Screenplay by Richard Harris

Produced by Jack Greenwood

Starring: Emrys Jones, Sarah Lawson, Patrick Barr, Garfield Morgan

Two criminals break into an office safe and steal some bonds. The alarm is sounded and their getaway driver disappears, leaving them to be chased through the London streets by the police, and caught.

Later, one of the criminals, Frank Stewart (Jones), escapes from prison just a month before he is due to be released because he needs to get the bonds before any of the other gang members do.

Some exciting scenes with the chase at the beginning, and a fight in a London sewer later on. For its time the film has some quite graphic violence.

Locations: no Merton Park locations but quite a bit of outside shooting, especially in the opening sequence as the gang are chased through London streets by police.

Notes: interesting to see two characters in roles that they would later be known for in other contexts. Garfield Morgan is a police inspector as he was to be in TV police series The Sweeney in the 1970s and Brian Wilde is a prison warder as he was to be in TV comedy series Porridge – also in the 1970s.

RETURN TO SENDER (1963)

Directed by Gordon Hales

Screenplay by John Roddick

Produced by Jack Greenwood

Starring: Nigel Davenport, Yvonne Romain, Geoffrey Keen, William Russell

Dino Steffano (Davenport) is just about to set sail on his boat when the police arrive to arrest him for fraud. He finds that the prosecuting barrister is Robert Lindley (Keen), whom he believes will secure a conviction so he has to somehow undermine his credibility and plans to compromise him with the aid of glamorous Lisa Maxwell (Romain). He uses accomplice Mike Cochrane (Russell) to take compromising photos, but can he be trusted?

Locations: no Merton Park locations.

Notes: Nigel Davenport had appeared in small roles in prestigious films such as Look Back in Anger (1959) with Richard Burton and The Entertainer (1960) with Laurence Olivier. He went on to appear in Life at the Top (1965) with Laurence Harvey and A Man For All Seasons (1966) with Paul Scofield.

Geoffrey Keen went on to appear in several James Bond films in the 1970s and 80s.

Yvonne Romain appeared in Merton Park film Devil Doll (1964).

RICOCHET (1963)

Directed by John Llewellyn Moxey (The City of the Dead, Foxhole in Cairo)

Screenplay by Roger Marshall

Produced by Jack Greenwood

Starring: Maxine Audley, Richard Leech, Alex Scott, Dudley Foster

Solicitor Alan Phipps (Leech) makes a strange deal with his wife Yvonne's ex-lover to blackmail her. He manages to persuade Yvonne (Audley) to meet ex-lover John Brodie (Scott) at a hotel and to take a gun with her which she believes only contains blank ammunition and is simply to frighten him. Phipp's plan is perhaps more devious than Brodie had bargained for.

This film was made in the heavy winter of 1962/3 and the snow adds to the atmosphere of the unsettling relationships between the main players. Even the police inspector, Cummins (Patrick Magee) is a rather threatening presence.

Locations: no Merton Park locations, but the nearby, and now defunct, Streatham ice rink is used in a couple of scenes only adding to the wintry atmosphere.

Notes: In 1960 Maxine Audley had starred in Michael Powell's controversial film Peeping Tom (1960). She also appeared in a couple of other Edgar Wallace episodes as well as the final episode of Merton Park's Scales of Justice series, Payment in Kind (1967).

Three years after this Alex Scott appeared in Fahrenheit 451 (1966) with Julie Christie.

Richard Leech had appeared in The Good Companions (1957) with Celia Johnson and later in Gandhi (1982) with Ben Kingsley and John Gielgud.

THE DOUBLE (1963)

Directed by Lionel Harris (Guilty Party, Position of Trust)

Screenplay by John Roddick, Lindsay Galloway

Produced by Jack Greenwood

Starring: Alan MacNaughtan, Jeanette Sterk, Robert Brown

John Cleeve (MacNaughtan) arrives back in UK from South Africa in a wheelchair and claims to have lost his memory, though he believes he killed his business partner, Derreck, out there. John's friend Mary (Sterk) gets a job with a man named Derreck who resembles John's old business partner – but is it him? When John starts to get his memory back he believes that *his* name is Derreck!

A rather convoluted plot, but reasonably entertaining.

Locations: no Merton Park locations.

Notes: Jeanette Sterk had appeared in The Prisoner (1955) with Alec Guinness and Lust for Life (1956) with Kirk Douglas.

Robert Brown appeared in several James Bond films as M.

THE RIVALS (1963)

Directed by Max Varnel (Moment of Indiscretion, Mrs Gibbons' Boys, Return of a Stranger)

Screenplay by John Roddick

Produced by Jack Greenwood

Starring: Jack Gwillim, Erica Rogers, Brian Smith

A gang of car thieves find that the car they have stolen contains a ransom note for the recently kidnapped daughter of wealthy businessman Rolf Nielsen (Gwillim). They decide to capitalise on this bit of serendipity but the kidnappers aren't going to make it easy for them.

A very good episode with strong central performances, some colourful minor characters and an intriguing plot.

Locations: lots of outside shooting – in central London and also many locations in and around Merton Park, including Wimbledon Common, Wimbledon Chase, and Circle Gardens, Kenley Road and Poplar Road in Merton Park. Unusually, a real road name, Barham Road in Raynes Park, is used in the script.

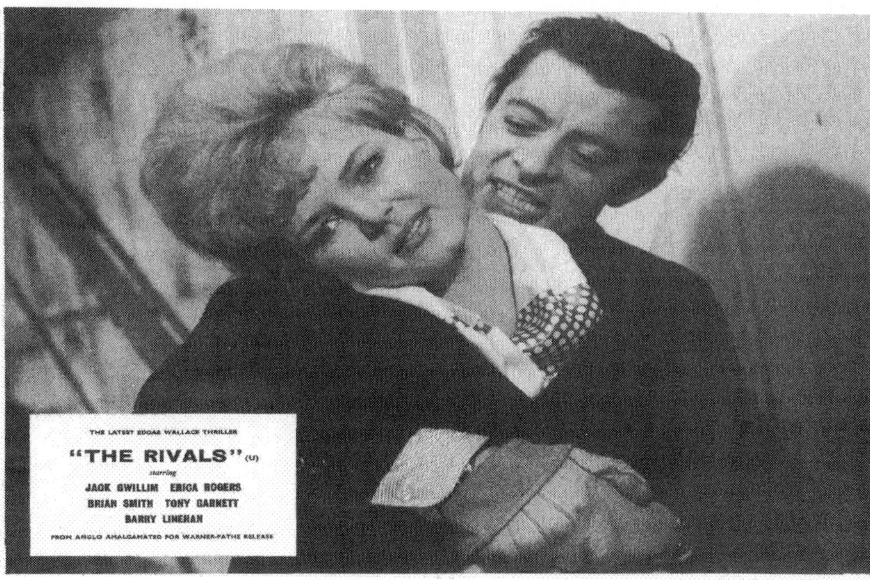

TO HAVE AND TO HOLD (1963)

Directed by Herbert Wise (I, Claudius, TV series – 1976, Breaking the Code, TV film – 1996)

Screenplay by Jimmy Sangster

Produced by Jack Greenwood

Starring: Ray Barrett, Katharine Blake, Nigel Stock, William Hartnell

Another very good episode, with Ray Barrett playing detective Henry Fraser who becomes romantically linked with a woman who believes her ex-boyfriend is trying to kill her. The woman, Claudia (Blake) is married, and Fraser has a girlfriend, so it gets complicated. When Fraser's boss, Inspector Roberts (Hartnell) finds out about their liaison he takes Fraser off the case, but Fraser starts to become even more involved, with disastrous consequences.

A taut thriller that packs a lot of story into under an hour and keeps the viewer guessing throughout. Is Claudia genuine? Does her story stack up? Can Fraser believe what she is telling him?

Locations: no Merton Park locations, but quite a bit of filming in Bournemouth where the story is partly set.

Notes: Later that year (1963) William Hartnell made TV history by becoming the first Doctor Who. Ray Barrett was a familiar face on TV, particularly in the 1960s and 70s and even appeared in a couple of 1965 episodes of Dr Who with William Hartnell. He had also been in the earlier episode of the Edgar Wallace series, Time to Remember (1962).

This was the first film directed by Herbert Wise, who was mainly known as a TV director.

Screenwriter Jimmy Sangster wrote and produced many Hammer horror films and was also an uncredited writer on Merton Park's The Criminal (1960).

THE PARTNER (1963)

Directed by Gerald Glaister

Screenplay by John Roddick

Produced by Jack Greenwood

Starring: Yoko Tani, Guy Doleman, Ewan Roberts, Anthony Booth

Actress Lin Siyan (Tani) becomes involved in tax avoidance at the film studios where she is working when she is paid £2000 (over £40,000 in 2019) cash in hand. The accountant who paid her, Briers (Noel Johnson) is later found dead in a fish tank at the film studios. Film director Wayne Douglas (Doleman) wants to find out if Briars was murdered and hires a private detective.

Locations: the streets local to Merton Park studios had often been used for location shooting, but this time it was even closer to home – the studios themselves! As the plot revolved around a film studio what better place to use? And it gives fans a rare opportunity to see what Merton Park studios looked like both inside and out. When a car drives through the gates the sign reading Merton Park Studios can clearly be seen.

Notes: Japanese actress Yoko Tani had appeared in The Savage Innocents (1960) with Anthony Quinn and in My Geisha (1962) with Shirley MacLaine and Edward G Robinson and was later in Merton Park sci-fi film Invasion (1966).

Three years after this (1966) Anthony Booth was to become better known as Alf Garnett's son-in-law Mike Rawlins in TV comedy series Till Death Us Do Part. In real life he became well-known again in the 1990s as father-in-law of Prime Minister Tony Blair.

ACCIDENTAL DEATH (1963)

Directed by Geoffrey Nethercott (Dead of Night, Merry Christmas Mr Lawrence)

Screenplay by Arthur La Bern

Produced by Jack Greenwood

Starring: Richard Vernon, John Carson, Derrick Sherwin, Jacqueline Ellis

Henriette (Ellis) is living at the house of her guardian, Johnnie Paxton (Vernon) when one night there is a prowler in the grounds. Henriette sends her boyfriend Alan (Sherwin) out to investigate, and he has a fight with the intruder. When Johnnie appears he recognises the intruder as Paul Lanson (Carson) whom he knew from the war.

Paul is invited to stay at the house but later tells Johnnie he is there to kill him to avenge members of his family that Johnnie betrayed to the Nazis. Paul becomes an almost Pinteresque menacing outsider who shatters the peace of the household, even making a play for Henriette.

It is a good episode and has many dramatic moments, but is slightly diluted by Johnnie's diffidence in the face of death threats.

Locations: Merton Park railway station is used, but renamed Aldbury Halt. Merton Park garage is featured, as is nearby Wilson Hospital in Mitcham (now closed).

Notes: Richard Vernon appeared in many high-profile films. The same year as this he appeared in The Servant (1963) with Dirk Bogarde, and the following year in both Goldfinger and A Hard Day's Night. He had also appeared in a couple of the other Edgar Wallace episodes, The Clue of the Twisted Candle (1960) and The Share Out (1962).

FIVE TO ONE (1963)

Directed by Gordon Flemyng (The Split, Dr Who and the Daleks, The Great Catherine)

Screenplay by Roger Marshall

Produced by Jack Greenwood

Starring: John Thaw, Lee Montague, Ingrid Hafner, Brian McDermott

Alan Roper (Thaw) is planning a robbery but wants to be able to launder the money afterwards. He strikes a deal with bent bookie Larry Hart (Montague) who will give him just £12,000 of the robbery's anticipated £60,000 proceeds – hence the 'five to one' of the title.

Roper and his accomplices, girlfriend Pat (Hafner) and friend John (McDermott) plan also to rob Larry Hart to improve on the 'five to one' he has offered.

A very good episode with lots of twists and turns along the way, plenty of drama and intrigue. Although playing a villain in this John Thaw's Roper has more than a touch of the uncompromising Jack Regan character he was to play in 70s police series The Sweeney.

Locations: quite a lot of location shooting that looks like South London, but strangely, not Merton Park.

Notes: director Gordon Flemyng, later known for work on the Avengers and Dr Who had the previous year directed another Wallace episode, Solo For Sparrow which included a then unknown Michael Caine.

DOWNFALL (1964)

Directed by John Llewellyn Moxey (The City of the Dead, Foxhole in Cairo)

Screenplay by Robert Banks Stewart

Produced by Jack Greenwood

Starring: Maurice Denham, Nadja Rejin, TP McKenna, Peter Barkworth

Brilliant barrister Sir Harold Crossley (Denham) succeeds in getting Martin Somers (McKenna) off a murder charge when everyone else believes he is guilty. Sir Harold has an attractive, much younger wife, Suzanne (Rejin) whom he would like to get rid of but doesn't want to divorce. He then decides to employ Somers as a chauffeur and general factotum in the hope that he will have an affair with his wife and he can begin a relationship with a female barrister he has his eyes on.

Everyone thinks he is mad to employ Somers – especially when he goes away for a few days and leaves them both alone at home.

Locations: Merton Park garage, Westway in nearby Raynes Park, the Apple Market and Griffin pub in nearby Kingston, the Telegraph pub at Putney Heath and York House Garden at Twickenham.

Notes: Maurice Denham had been in Two Way Stretch (1960) with Peter Sellers and Damn the Defiant (1962) with Alec Guinness and was later to appear in Day of the Jackal (1981) with Edward Fox. Also, in a role not entirely dissimilar to this one he played a judge who ends up in prison in TV comedy series Porridge (1977) with Ronnie Barker. He had also appeared in another Edgar Wallace film, The Set Up (1963).

TP McKenna went on to much bigger things, appearing in Anne of the Thousand Days (1969), Straw Dogs (1971), and Britannia Hospital (1982).

THE VERDICT (1964)

Directed by David Eady (Faces in the Dark, Where's Johnny?)

Screenplay by Arthur La Bern

Produced by Jack Greenwood

Starring: Nigel Davenport, Cec Linder, Zena Marshall, Paul Stassino

Crook Joe Armstrong (Linder) is deported back to the UK where he faces a murder charge from twenty years previously. One of the first people he meets is Larry Mason (Davenport) who had managed to keep him out of jail last time he was here, but now there is a new gangland boss, Danny Thorne (Stassino) who runs protection rackets in London and doesn't want Armstrong getting involved again.

There is plenty going on, with the police pursuing Armstrong and his attempts to re-establish himself as 'King of the Underworld' as Thorne now styles himself. And can he trust Mason, or indeed his own glamorous girlfriend, Carola (Marshall)?

Locations: no Merton Park locations.

Notes: that same year Cec Linder had appeared in Goldfinger (1964) and a couple of years previously had appeared in Kubrick's Lolita (1962) with James Mason and Shelley Winters.

Zena Marshall had also appeared in Bond film, Goldfinger (1964).

WE SHALL SEE (1964)

Directed by Quentin Lawrence (The Crawling Eye, Playback)

Screenplay by Donal Giltinan

Produced by Jack Greenwood

Starring: Maurice Kaufmann, Faith Brook, Alex MacIntosh, Alec Mango

Neurotic and unpredictable Alva Collins (Brook) attempts to make her pilot husband Evan (Kaufmann) give up flying and when he drives off in a rage after an argument crashes his car and spends weeks in hospital where he is attracted to a nurse, Rosemary (Bridget Armstrong).

Alva's brother Greg (MacIntosh) is at their house hoping to get some inheritance money from Alva, left by their late parents, but will Alva cooperate? She also has a severe allergy to bee stings, and when her gardener Ludo (Mango) introduces a hive to their garden she tells him he is sacked.

When a swarm of bees is let into Alva's bedroom while she is asleep the audience is spoilt for choice as to who did it. For some reason, the director missed the opportunity to show a Hitchcockian horror scene of Alva's terrifying encounter with the bees, which, with her previous unhinged performances, could have been a centrepiece of the film.

Locations: no Merton Park locations.

Notes: Faith Brook appeared in North Sea Hijack (1980) with Roger Moore and James Mason, Eye of the Needle (1981) with Donald Sutherland, and Razor's Edge (1984) with Bill Murray.

WHO WAS MADDOX? (1964)

Directed by Geoffrey Nethercott

Screenplay by Roger Marshall

Produced by Jack Greenwood

Starring: Bernard Lee, Jack Watling, Suzanne Lloyd, Finlay Currie

There is a burglary at the home of Jack and Diane Heath (Watling and Lloyd) and Diane takes the opportunity to hide some of her jewellery and claim it has been stolen. Then Jack gets a telephone call to say that his uncle Alec (Currie), who is also his boss, has been murdered while tackling a burglar.

The call has come from a policeman named Maddox. When Jack goes to the house he finds his uncle still alive – so who was Maddox, and what was the reason for the call?

Locations: no Merton Park locations.

Notes: Jack Watling had appeared in many films before this, including The Winslow Boy (1948) with Robert Donat, and Reach for the Sky (1956) with Kenneth More. Finlay Currie, born in 1878, had appeared in many, many films, including The Good Companions (1932) with John Gielgud, Great Expectations (1946) with John Mills, Ben Hur (1959) with Charlton Heston, and, just the year before this, Billy Liar (1962) with Tom Courtenay.

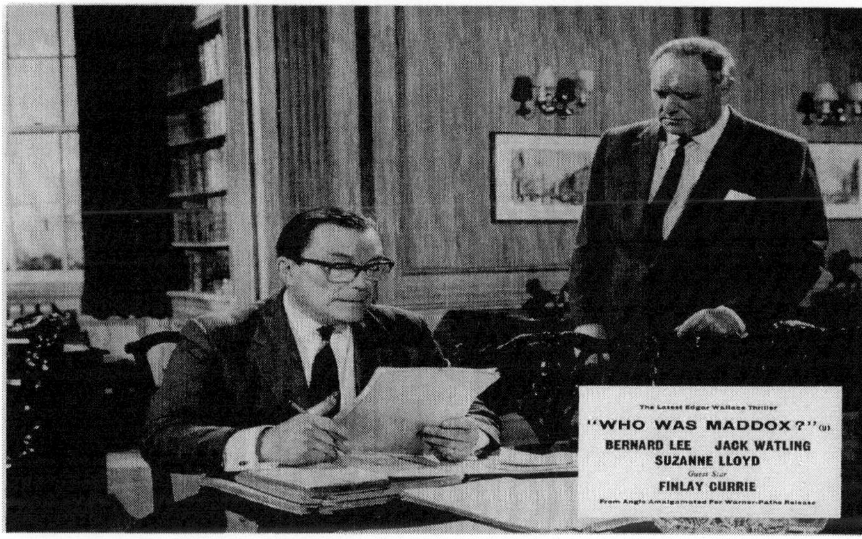

FACE OF A STRANGER (1964)

Directed by John Llewellyn Moxey

Screenplay by Jimmy Sangster

Produced by Jack Greenwood

Starring: Jeremy Kemp, Rosemary Leach, Philip Locke, Jean Marsh

A very good episode with a much more modern feel than some of the others. John Bell (Locke) is about to be released from prison when he is found with a knife and loses remission. When his cellmate Vince Howard (Kemp) is released Bell asks him to look in on his wife Mary, who is blind, to check if she is all right.

When Vince is given the brush-off by his own wife, Grace (Marsh), he moves in with Mary, letting her think he is her husband. He also plans to go and collect the money from the robbery that got John into prison.

Very good acting, believable characters and interesting camera work including the use of hand-held camera helped to make this a gripping episode.

Locations: No Merton Park locations but quite a lot of outside filming including modern flats, railway stations etc.

Notes: Jimmy Sangster was one of the main writers of screenplays for Hammer horror films including Curse of Frankenstein (1957), Blood of the Vampire (1958) and The Mummy (1959). Also, he wrote the story for another Merton Park film, The Criminal (1960) starring Stanley Baker, though the screenplay was by Alun Owen.

Jeremy Kemp went on to appear in A Bridge Too Far (1977) with Sean Connery, The Prisoner of Zenda (1979) with Peter Sellers and Four Weddings and a Funeral (1994) with Hugh Grant.

Jean Marsh became a household name through her role as Rose in TV series Upstairs, Downstairs (1971–75). She had also appeared in Merton Park's The Limping Man (1953) – her screen debut.

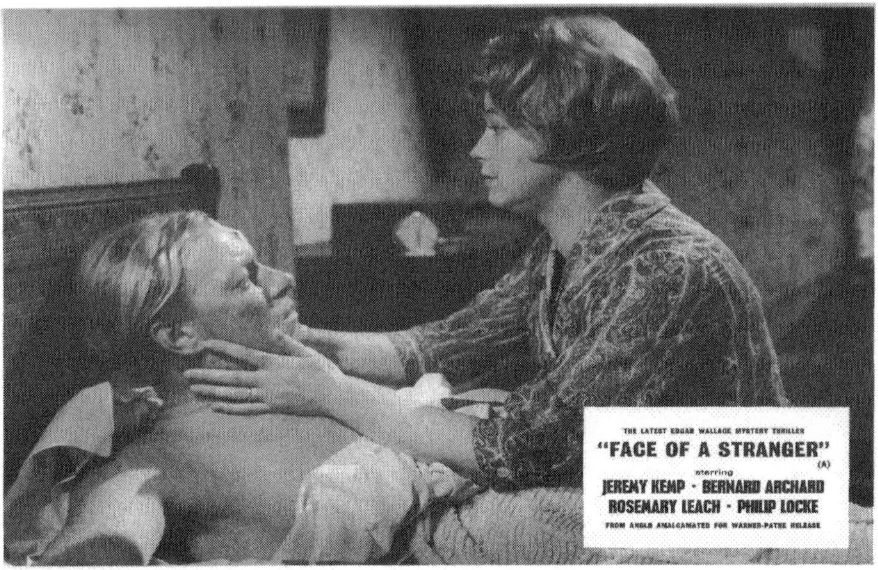

ACT OF MURDER (1964)

Directed by Alan Bridges (The Hireling, The Shooting Party, Out of Season)

Screenplay by Lewis Davidson

Produced by Jack Greenwood

Starring: Justine Lord, Anthony Bate, John Carson, Dandy Nicholls

Ralph Longman (Bate) and his ex-actress wife Ann (Lord) are doing a house swap for two weeks with a couple in London. Their friend Tim Ford (Carson) has been visiting and trying to persuade Ann to do some acting work again. As soon as the Longmans have gone the other couple start loading their valuables into an antiques dealer's van. However, they are disturbed when Tim returns for a bag he's forgotten.

When the Longmans come back they find everything as they left it, apart from their chickens, which are now dead. Something strange is going on, but what, exactly?

Locations: no Merton Park locations.

Notes: Dandy Nichols had been in the business since the 1940s and was to become most famous for her role as the long-suffering wife of Alf Garnett in TV comedy series Till Death Us Do Part (1966–75). She also appeared in many films, including The Bed-sitting Room (1969) with Peter Cook and Ralph Richardson, O Lucky Man (1973) with Malcolm McDowell and, the same year as this film, another Merton Park film, The Leather Boys (1964) with Rita Tushingham. The following year she also appeared in the Beatles film Help (1965) and The Knack and How to Get It (1965) with Michael Crawford and Rita Tushingham.

NEVER MENTION MURDER (1964)

Directed by John Nelson Burton (TV series Ghost Squad, Emergency Ward 10, etc.)

Screenplay by Robert Banks Stewart

Produced by Jack Greenwood

Starring: Dudley Foster, Maxine Audley, Michael Coles, Pauline Yates

Heart Surgeon Philip Teasdale (Foster) finds that his wife Liz (Audley) has been having an affair with Tony Sorbo (Coles) and employs a private detective named Carstairs (Brian Haines) to follow them, though after getting some initial information, suddenly dispenses with his services.

When Tony has a stroke during his mind-reading stage act the heart surgeon who has to deal with him is none other than Philip Teasdale. The indiscreet and unscrupulous Carstairs now decides to use the information he has found to his own advantage.

A gripping episode with Foster's character alternating between caring surgeon and vindictive, cuckolded husband, and Haines' detective managing to be both smarmy and intimidating.

Locations: no Merton Park locations.

Notes: this was the only film that John Nelson Burton directed, the rest of his work being in TV, but one critic commented that 'the film is often directed with an astonishing degree of visual flair.'

Dudley Foster was a well-known face on TV in the 1960s often portraying either policemen or villains in series such as Danger Man, Z-Cars, The Saint and the Avengers. The previous year he had appeared in another Merton Park Edgar Wallace film, Ricochet (1963).

THE MAIN CHANCE (1964)

Directed by John Knight (Avengers, Armchair Theatre)

Screenplay by Richard Harris

Produced by Jack Greenwood

Starring: Gregoire Aslan, Edward de Souza, Tracy Reed, Stanley Meadows

Michael Blake (de Souza) is an ex-pilot, gambler and man–about-town who gets headhunted by criminal mastermind Potter (Aslan) to fly in some diamonds. He had at first refused the job, but Potter 'persuaded' him. Will Blake do the job as planned or double-cross him?

Potter comes across almost like a Bond villain with his secret lair full of computers only accessible through a door masquerading as a bookcase. He also has CCTV on his premises which was probably not commonplace in 1964.

A good yarn with quite a bit of action and strong performances from the main actors.

Notes: This was the last film to be directed by John Knight before his death in 1967.

GAME FOR THREE LOSERS (1965)

Directed by Gerry O'Hara (Amsterdam Affair, All the Right Noises, The Bitch)

Screenplay by Roger Marshall (based on the novel by Edgar Lustgarten)

Produced by Jack Greenwood

Starring: Michael Gough, Mark Eden, Toby Robins, Rachel Gurney

MP Robert Hilary (Gough) employs new secretary Frances (Robins) and before long they are kissing in the office. When Frances' criminal boyfriend Oliver (Eden) finds out he sees it as a good opportunity for blackmail.

Hilary pays to begin with but then tells his solicitor who suggests taking Oliver to court and yet still maintaining his anonymity. The judge, unfortunately, has other ideas.

A good cast, especially Alan Cuthbertson as the defending lawyer who runs rings round the MP in court.

Locations: no Merton Park locations.

Notes: Rachel Gurney, who plays the wife of Michael Gough, had an actress daughter by the name of Sharon Gurney who, in real life, married Gough's son, Simon.

A couple of years before this Gerry O'Hara had been assistant director on Tom Jones (1963) starring Albert Finney.

It was strange that this Edgar Lustgarten story hadn't been used as the basis for one of the Scales of Justice series which he had hosted. It was first published in 1952.

CHANGE PARTNERS (1965)

Directed by Robert Lynn (Dr Crippen, Coast of Skeletons, Killer's Carnival)

Screenplay by Donal Giltinan

Produced by Jack Greenwood

Starring: Zena Walker, Anthony Dawson, Kenneth Cope, Basil Henson

Businessman Ricky Gallen (Henson) is having an affair with Anna Arkwright (Zena Walker) but both of them are married and Zena persuades Ricky to take drastic action so they can be together.

In the meantime, conman Joe Trent (Cope) has been spying on the pair and plans to blackmail Ricky.

Locations: no Merton Park locations.

Notes: Robert Lynn went on to be one of the second unit directors on the first two Superman films (1978 and 1980).

Zena Walker appeared in Cromwell (1970) with Richard Harris and Alec Guinness and The Dresser (1983) with Albert Finney and Tom Courtenay.

Anthony Dawson had been in Hitchcock's Dial M For Murder (1954) with Ray Milland and Grace Kelly. Also, a couple of years before this film he had played Blofeld in From Russia With Love (1963). He had also appeared in Dr No (1962).

STRANGLER'S WEB (1965)

Directed by John Llewellyn Moxey

Screenplay by George Baxt

Produced by Jack Greenwood

Starring: John Stratton, Pauline Munro, Gerald Harper, Griffith Jones

It starts with a frightened woman being pursued through undergrowth before being killed by someone unseen.

Her slovenly, heavy drinking and violent husband is the prime suspect as she has been strangled by a type of cord he uses in his work.

The lawyer engaged to defend him however is also a drinker and a wife-beater who believes his story.

A quirky story with some unusual characters and a touch of the horror film here and there. Some witty dialogue and interesting camera work make this a very watchable addition to the Edgar Wallace series.

Locations: Church Road and Dog & Fox pub, Wimbledon Village High Street.

Notes: George Baxt had also written the screenplay for Circus of Horrors (1960) which, like this film, featured facial disfigurement.

Griffith Jones had appeared in Henry V (1944) with Laurence Olivier, and Miranda (1948) with Glynis Johns and Googie Withers.

Gerald Harper was to become famous the following year as the eponymous hero in the TV series Adam Adamant Lives! (1966–67). The series was co-created by Richard Harris, writer of several of the Edgar Wallace episodes in this series.

DEAD MAN'S CHEST (1965)

Directed by Patrick Dromgoole (Machinegunner, Thick as Thieves – both TV films)

Screenplay by Donal Giltinan

Produced by Jack Greenwood

Starring: John Thaw, Graham Crowden, Peter Bowles

David Jones and his friend Johnnie Gordon plan a hoax to draw attention to the police's sometime reliance on circumstantial evidence and also to create a publicity stunt which they hope will bring them media attention – and money. Johnnie is put into a wooden chest after having been hit by David to create some blood, David then drives the chest off in his van to plant it somewhere and claim there has been a murder.

Unfortunately the van is stolen by some bungling bank robbers to use as a getaway vehicle.

David tells the police, but they've been the victim of his stories before and don't investigate. No one knows where Johnnie and the chest are now but they assume he is dead, having suffocated.

The nearest to a comedy the series ever got and it does feature several actors later known for comedy roles: Peter Bowles, Michael Robbins and Graham Crowden.

Crowden is excellent as the devious and scheming newspaper editor, and Robbins, as Sergeant Harris, creates an amusing cross-talking double act with John Collin as Inspector Briggs. Peter Bowles is the whiney-voiced cockney leader of the gang of hopeless bank robbers.

All good fun, but John Thaw still manages to keep the tension going as he faces a murder charge.

Locations: fittingly, as the last in the series, an aerial panning shot of Merton Park studios is shown – along with the studio's favourite pub, The Leather Bottle, next door.

Notes: John Thaw's first credited role in a film had been the previous Edgar Wallace episode Five to One (1963).

The year after this film was made Peter Bowles appeared in iconic 60s British film Blow Up (1966) with David Hemmings – who had been a child star of another Merton Park film, Five Clues to Fortune (1957).

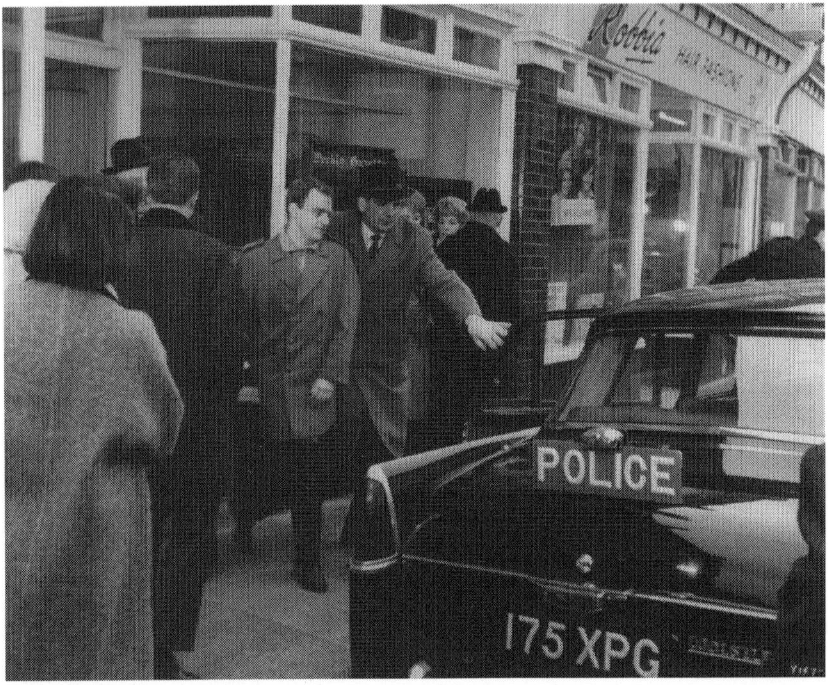

John Thaw getting arrested at Merton Park Parade (from Dead Man's Chest) just opposite Merton Park studios

FILMS MADE AT MERTON PARK AFTER 1967

Although many sources claim that production at Merton Park studios ceased in 1967, or even 1966 (see 'Myths' section) there is ample evidence to show that some filming work was still going on here until at least 1972.

The BFI lists two CFF (Children's Film Foundation) titles made here after 1967: Egghead's Robot (1970) and The Troublesome Double (1971), both starring child actor Keith Chegwin (see separate entry).

But there was also the thriller/horror film The Corpse (aka Crucible of Horror) (see separate entry) starring Michael Gough who had appeared in several other films made at Merton Park (Konga, Horrors of the Black Museum, and a couple of the Edgar Wallace films). This was released in 1971 so was presumably shot in 1970.

Also, the 1969 film Women in Love starring Oliver Reed, Glenda Jackson and Alan Bates was partly filmed at Merton Park. The cinematographer of the film, Billy Williams, explains in an online filmed interview that after the infamous nude wrestling scene had been completed the director, Ken Russell, realised that some more filming needed to be done, but the original location, Elvaston Castle in Derbyshire, was no longer available. It was therefore decided that Merton Park Studios would be used for that and a few other scenes.

An interesting footnote to this story is that Rank refused to distribute the film because of this scene and it was put out instead by the rival ABC chain. J Arthur Rank had of course started his career at Merton Park in 1934 with the religious film Mastership (see separate entry).

Women in Love also had in the cast Merton Park stalwart Michael Gough playing Mr Brangwen.

The latest film with Merton Park connections also starred Michael Gough. It was the horror film Horror Hospital (1973). This was filmed in 1972 and according to the end credits was made 'on location and at Merton Park.' Also, according to Robin Askwith, who starred in the film, some shooting was done at Merton Park studios, mainly the pop group scene. In addition to this the railway scenes were filmed at the old Merton Park railway station.

Robin Askwith has also said that a school scene in the film If (1968) was made at Merton Park studios. This film was directed by Lindsay Anderson who had made a short documentary film Meet the Pioneers at Merton Park studios in 1948, his first film.

Incidentally, the film If also had one other local connection, one of the locations was close to Merton Park studios: the Broadway Motor Co shop in Gladstone Road (which is now the Wetherspoons pub, Wibbas Down).

It seems then that contrary to popular opinion the studios were being used well into the 1970s, at least five years longer than has been hitherto thought.

MERTON PARK MYTHS

Over the years one or two myths have attached themselves to Merton Park studios and once established seem to take on a life of their own, spreading on the internet like bindweed.

PAYMENT IN KIND

Many websites will tell you that the last film made at Merton Park Studios was Payment in Kind starring John Thaw in 1967. The only problems are that Payment in Kind wasn't the last film made at Merton Park, it wasn't made in 1967 and it didn't star John Thaw. In fact, he wasn't in it at all.

Payment in Kind was the last of the thirteen episodes of Scales of Justice and was released in March 1967 but had been made in 1966. John Thaw had appeared in a couple of the Edgar Wallace mysteries made at Merton Park (Five To One and Dead Man's Chest, released in 1963 and 1965 respectively) but he didn't appear in any of the Scales of Justice series. Also, several other films were made at Merton Park studios after 1967 as detailed elsewhere in this book.

CARRY ON SERGEANT

One or two websites will tell you that the first of the Carry On series, Carry On Sergeant, was made at Merton Park studios. This piece of misinformation seems to come from the misreading of a reference in the book British 'B' Film' by Steve Chibnall and Brian McFarlane in which they talk about Merton Park being in a partnership with Insignia Films but it was the latter company that made Carry On Sergeant (at Pinewood Studios).

JOHNNY YOU'RE WANTED

Again, some websites will say that this 1956 film starring John Slater and Alfred Marks was made at Merton Park but it was actually shot at Nettlefold Studios in Walton-On-Thames. The misunderstanding may have come about because the director was Vernon Sewell, who had directed several films at Merton Park, including Ghost Ship (1952), Counterspy (1953) and Dangerous Voyage (1954).

RADIO LUXEMBOURG

A couple of websites say 'for a time it (Merton Park studios) was home to Radio Luxembourg.' No evidence can be found for this claim and online histories of the radio station do not confirm it either. However, in the documentary Remembering Merton Park studios (2008, directed by Ken Rowles) it is stated that Radio Luxembourg used recording facilities here.

WIMBLEDON

When the studios are mentioned online or in print it is quite often as 'Merton Park studios, Wimbledon.' As the name implies, the studios were in Merton Park, not Wimbledon. The back of the studios was admittedly extremely close to the parish boundary line, but definitely still within Merton Park.

EMMA HAMILTON

More than one source has claimed that Long Lodge, the 18th century building at the front of the studios in Kingston Road, was once the home of Emma Hamilton. She never lived here, but was not far away at Merton Place (near the present Nelson Arms pub in Merton High Street) from 1801–1805. This misunderstanding possibly dates back to an interview film producer John Croydon gave to Kinematograph Weekly on 13/12/62 in which he says 'for a long time I was under the illusion that the ghosts of Lord Nelson and Lady Hamilton flitted through it' (Long Lodge). However, he goes on to say 'Unfortunately ... the Nelson myth has been exploded by an examination of the records.'

MARTIN SCORSESE

According to the Wikipedia entry for Horrors of the Black Museum there is a copy of the film in the Museum of Modern Art, New York, at the behest of Martin Scorsese. It's a tantalising prospect but unfortunately MOMA know nothing about it. The story seems to come from an interview the film's producer, Herman Cohen, gave to Tom Weaver (published in 1994) in which he says film directors Scorsese, Spielberg and George Lucas were donating forty films to MOMA and that they wanted Horrors of the Black Museum to be among them as they all grew up on it and loved it and thought that a lot of inventive things were done in the film. Along with Stephen Spielberg, George Lucas and others Scorsese did set up the Film Foundation at MOMA and it's possible that the idea of putting this film in the archive was discussed but it seems it never happened. It is however interesting that a low-budget film made at Merton Park was so highly regarded by these top Hollywood directors.

THE KRAYS

Some sources suggest that the Kray twins had a cameo role in Sparrows Can't Sing (1963) but no image of them in the film has ever been found and an interviewee on the 2017 DVD release of the film confirms they were not in it. They did however have some involvement in the film (see entry for Sparrows Can't Sing).

UNKNOWN ACTORS

There seems to have been a feeling among some critics of Merton Park studios that the films either used unknown actors or those whose careers were in decline.

This is far from the truth as actors who appeared in even the more modest of Merton Park productions, such as the Scotland Yard series, had done prestigious work both before and after their work here. For example, May Hallet, who appeared in Scotland Yard episode The Stateless Man (1955) had appeared in Powell and Pressburger's Black Narcissus (1947) alongside Deborah Kerr and Flora Robson then years later in the film of Terence Rattigan's Separate Tables (1958) with David Niven, Rita Hayworth and Deborah Kerr.

Similarly, when Peter Sellers starred in the Merton Park comedy short The Case of the Mukkinese Battlehorn (1956) he had already starred in The Ladykillers (1955) with Alec Guinness and Herbert Lom as well as several other films.

Incidentally, character actress Edie Martin appeared in several Ealing comedies (including The Ladykillers, starring Sellers) both before and after appearing in a small, uncredited role in The Mysterious Bullet (1955), one of Merton Park's Scotland Yard films.

ACKNOWLEDGEMENTS

Thanks to the following people who have been very helpful and generous with their time:

Ian Caunce

Jess Conrad OBE

Sarah Cronin-Stanley (Renown Films)

Michael Deeley

Robert Devcic

Kat Hubbard

Steve Lock (book layout)

David Moore (78rpm.co.uk)

Massimo Moretti (STUDIOCANAL Films Ltd)

Bruce Robertson

Ken Rowles

Robert Whichelow (front cover montage)

The following organisations have been useful sources of information:

BFI (British Film Institute)

IMDb (Internet Movie Database)

Merton Library Service

PHOTOGRAPHS

Permission to use the images in this book has been given by the following:

Front cover photo of studios and back cover photo, © London Borough of Merton

Front cover image of Konga, courtesy of STUDIOCANAL Films Ltd

The Admiral's Secret, Hindle Wakes, Death Goes to School, Narrowing Circle, The Limping Man, courtesy of Renown Films

The Case of the Mukkinese Battlehorn, courtesy of Michael Deeley

Hidden Homicide, '© Paramount Pictures Corp. All Rights Reserved.'

Devil Doll, Projected Man, Horror Hospital, courtesy of Screenbound International Pictures

The Atomic Man, The Brain Machine, Confession, Crime of Honour, The Counterfeit Plan, The Criminal, Dead Man's Chest, Dangerous Voyage, The Drayton Case, The Electronic Monster, Face of a Stranger, Ghost Ship, The Headless Ghost, Horrors of the Black Museum, The Hypnotist, Incident at Midnight, Invasion, The Key Man, Konga, Late Night Final, Little Red Monkey, Man in the Shadow, Mysterious Bullet, Murder Anonymous, Print of Death, The Rivals, Solo For Sparrow, Sparrows Can't Sing, Strange Awakening, Street of Shadows, The Undesirable Neighbour, Who Was Maddox, courtesy of STUDIOCANAL Films Ltd

Advertisements from Kinematograph Weekly (pages 26, 41, 99, 103, 107, 108), courtesy of Time Inc. (UK) Ltd

BIBLIOGRAPHY

Attack of the Monster Movie Makers by Tom Weaver

Britain's First TV/Film Crime Series and the Industrialisation of its Film Industry by Dr Dave Mann

The British 'B' Film by Steve Chibnall and Brian McFarlane

An Autobiography of British Cinema by Brian McFarlane

Sixties British Cinema by Brian Murphy

The Children's Film Foundation by Robert Shail

Sidney J Furie: Life and Films by Daniel Kremer

POSTSCRIPT

Most of the films made at Merton Park, including all the Scotland Yard, Scales of Justice and Edgar Wallace series are available on DVD. Also, many of the films are regularly featured on the Talking Pictures channel on TV and are occasionally shown on other channels. Some of the documentary shorts made at Merton Park can be seen on the BFI website.